Women on the way Up

The Inspiring True Story of How
One Woman's Mentoring Program
Changed the Lives of
Young Underserved Women
in Profound and Lasting Ways

Laura Sheinkopf

Mindful Living Press 2016

© 2016 Joan Karff.

All rights reserved. No part of this book may be used or reproduced in any manner whatsoever without the written permission of the publisher. Published in the United States of America. For information, contact 800 West Avenue, Suite C-1, Miami Beach, FL 33139.

The use of quotations in this book is intended for illustrative purposes only and not to suggest affiliation, connection, or association between this book and the identified source of the quotation.

Cover Design: Cathy Gibbs Thornton

Library of Congress Control Number: 2016908558

ISBN: 0-9773455-5-6

Copy Editor: Melissa Hayes

For information about bulk discounts, please send inquiries to Scott Rogers at contact@mindfulliving.net

First Printing, May 2016

This book is dedicated
to every child
whose life could be inspired by a mentor.
May you find your mentor.
May you find your muse.

TABLE OF CONTENTS

Acknowledgments ix

Preface xi

Introduction 1

Chapter 1: Biography of a Mentor 3

Chapter 2: How and Why Women on the Way Up Works 19

Chapter 3: WOWU's Place in Education 33

Chapter 4: The Legacy of an Uncommon Woman 39

Chapter 5: Alumnae Profiles 43

A Message from Joan Karff 85

Appendix: Content Objectives 87

Sample Syllabus 95

Leadership & Board 99

With Gratitude

Joan Karff

Acknowledgments

I would like to thank the following individuals who have made Women on the Way Up (WOWU) what it is today, and who have helped to describe the program in this book.

Regina Rogers

I thank Regina for the generosity she has shown every good cause in the city of Houston and Beaumont, including WOWU. The creation of this book was Regina's idea, and she pursued this project with unfailing interest and passion. She also enlisted Ann Boor, who assisted with editing.

Ashley Brantley

A 2004 graduate of Lamar High School and WOWU, Ashley has followed the progress of this mentoring group with helpful enthusiasm. She has gathered all of the preliminary information about our alumnae and given much thought to this project. Although busy completing law school studies, Ashley compiled my personal history and chronicled all of the activities of the program with diligence and devotion.

Dr. James McSwain

As principal of Lamar High School, Dr. McSwain always has been in our corner. He has been attentive to the needs and importance of WOWU and has never failed to go the extra mile in making sure each aspect of the program was successful.

Ray Reiner

In his role in 2001 as superintendent of the Central District of the Houston Independent School District, Ray gave this program its start and was constantly encouraging and helpful. As president of the WOWU board, he has been a cherished and dependable partner, efficiently handling the financial aspects of the organization.

Dr. Gary Patterson

Both as a music educator and an indispensable administrator of the Houston Independent School District, Dr. Patterson has assumed the role of liaison between the school and our group. His love for the program is no less than mine. He has taken care of all the behind-the-scenes planning for each excursion and ensured that each outing was a delight.

Linda Harrison

In her job as counselor to the senior class, Linda has aided greatly in the identification of candidates for our program; she also oversees their schedules to make certain they have our time period free.

Pam Hsieh

As an administrative assistant, Pam handles all secretarial chores with sweetness and competence. She helps to process donations and manage all the details of our field trips.

Laura Sheinkopf

As an experienced professional, Laura has edited all of our program materials and has most competently compiled a thorough and readable account of WOWU.

Scott Rogers

When Regina thought to have this book become a reality, she looked to her nephew Scott to help assemble the pieces. Thank you, Scott, for working with Ashley Brantley and Laura Sheinkopf; for bringing on board Cathy Thornton, Melissa Hayes, and Christina Sava who did such wonderful jobs with the cover, interior design, and copyediting of the manuscript; and for seeing this project through to completion. We are so appreciative of the tremendous effort on Cathy's part to hunt down so very many of our alumnae and learn of their current career achievements.

To my family:
Sam Karff, Rachel Weissenstein, Amy Halevy, and Liz Seitz

I thank my most incredible husband for the love, strength, and encouragement he has shown me every day for fifty-six years. And I thank my daughters, whom I adore, and with whom I have shared each triumph and trial, always knowing I could count on their unwavering devotion.

Joan Karff
Houston, Texas
2016

Preface

This book is a brief account of Women on the Way Up (WOWU), a small mentoring program for young women in Houston, Texas. It is also an homage to the program's remarkable founder, Joan Karff. WOWU began in 2001 at Lamar High School, one of the oldest and one of the biggest high schools in the Houston Independent School District. Each year, ten students are chosen at the end of their junior year to participate in this yearlong program. Virtually all of the young women are minority students, and all are from underserved backgrounds. They are selected based on their previous school performance and their desire to attend college. Since its founding, nearly every graduate of WOWU has completed college, and many also have graduate degrees. WOWU was not modeled after any other program, and thus this book grew out of a widespread admiration for Karff and a desire to record her philosophy and methods in the hopes of inspiring others.

While the needs of public school students from financially disadvantaged families and crowded schools are great, WOWU demonstrates that a mentoring program can facilitate enormous emotional, intellectual, and social growth. Underserved students rarely have the opportunity to venture beyond the confines of the familial and communal realities into which they were born, but WOWU expands those horizons. In everything they read, in every person they meet, and in every experience they have as a group, students are expanding their awareness of the world and the opportunities that exist for them beyond the world to which they are accustomed.

Karff's philosophy proceeds with the assumption that education can be the bridge to a life of an individual's own choosing. She also assumes the responsibility of cultivating cultural awareness and the skills needed to navigate adult life successfully. WOWU is not a road map to success. It is instead a constellation of experiences that help students find an internal compass and the courage to press on.

There is something different about the kind of conversation that Karff is able to generate in her discussions with WOWU students. She elicits a love of learning that inspires students, and she actively listens to her students in ways that make them eager to participate. Essentially, she helps to instill intrinsic motivation within an expanding sphere of opportunity and challenge. WOWU is a learning experience that is exciting, challenging, and empowering. Karff wants her students not only to love learning, but also to be open to the new possibilities that learned people continue to discover as they move through life. Clearly, Karff sees "learned" as an applied attitude, a continuously refreshing perspective of the self and the world that emboldens. She was blessed by these advantages, and she believes that they are the reason she has been able to construct a rich and meaningful life. Even more importantly, Karff believes that a person who possesses the self-awareness, intellectual curiosity, and ability to reach out for help will be capable of overcoming a great many obstacles. In the wake of WOWU's success, it is hard to disagree.

Rabbi Laura Sheinkopf
Houston, Texas
May 2016

INTRODUCTION

Joan Karff spent the majority of her professional life in the world of dance, but instead of retiring when she left that world in 2000, she created a mentoring program for underserved young women in an inner-city urban high school. What follows is an account of how that program came to be, what it is today, and why it works.

Rather than presenting a curriculum and course outline, this book reveals the inside story of the program, including Karff's personal history, which has informed her methods. Later chapters provide an overview of the program's components and a look into the approach that makes this mentoring program, Women on the Way Up (WOWU), successful. The book's appendix offers guidance for those wishing to model a program on WOWU, including content objectives, a detailed discussion of subject matter covered by the program, and a sample syllabus.

College matriculation has long been the measure of success for programs that are aimed at underserved students, including WOWU. By that measure, WOWU has a staggering success rate. Nearly all participants in WOWU's yearlong program graduate from college, and many go on to earn graduate degrees. But these accolades are also indicators of tremendous intellectual and emotional growth, fostered in a variety of ways during their time with WOWU. This is not a program that seeks to improve academic skills or test scores per se; rather, it supports the social, emotional, and intellectual growth needed in order for young women to be effective advocates for themselves.

This brief account of Women on the Way Up also seeks to spotlight a truly inspiring and collaborative effort between a public school administration and a dedicated volunteer. While Karff created and drives WOWU, the program could not be what it is today without Lamar High School administration's support and active participation. The school ensures that the young women involved have no scheduling conflicts and allows the group to meet on campus during school hours. This saves a tremendous amount of time and resources that might otherwise burden the program and its participants.

Karff is not a remote intellectual despite her obvious and laudable intellect. She is not an eccentric artist despite her considerable artistic achievements and innate creativity. She is not a "Pollyanna," but she is a determined optimist. Given the success of her students, it's difficult to argue with her approach. Mentoring, in general, seems to harness the optimism of the individuals and institutions involved. While we look at test scores and grades to learn more about a school and a student's weaknesses, the solutions to the problems that lead to poor performance cannot always be found in the data. The solutions lie within the whole person and how that person comes to understand herself in relationship to her family, her school, and her world. Karff's mentoring through WOWU reaches out to the whole person.

A year spent with Karff and other "Women on the Way Up" discussing current events, literature, the arts, and the issues that directly affect young women has a profound impact on an individual's sense of herself and her place in the world. WOWU is proof that this well-rounded approach *does* translate into measurable academic and career success. It is our hope that this account will inform and inspire many similar programs around the nation.

Chapter One

Biography of a Mentor

Karff was born Joan G. Mag in 1936 in Connecticut. Her parents were Samuel Mag and Fanny Mittau Mag. The middle child of three, Joan had a younger brother and older sister; all three enjoyed a comfortable upbringing in the suburbs of New Britain, where her father ran a successful family clothing store called Mag and Sons. The Mags were of Jewish decent, but not observant, and both parents were intellectual and cultured. They worked hard and believed in giving back to their community.

Karff makes frequent references to Fanny because much of her philosophy on education and love of literature and the arts come directly from her mother. Fanny's paternal family were descendants of the German Jewish immigrants who came to the United States in the late nineteenth century seeking greater horizons. The German Jews saw America as a land of opportunity, and they flocked here with the expectation of being fully accepted as Americans. Fanny's maternal side of the family came to the United States from England in the 1850s. Her maternal grandfather fought for the Union in the Civil War. Fanny's parents were great lovers of music and culture.

Fanny did not have a privileged upbringing. She was born and raised in Hartford, Connecticut where her father made a living as a jeweler. Both of Fanny's parents were accomplished musicians. Her father played the violin and her mother was a pianist. The family was only nominally Jewish, but when Fanny was fourteen, her mother died and, in keeping with Jewish custom at the time, her father married his wife's surviving cousin. The home was a stable environment, but the family struggled financially; they could not afford to send Fanny to college.

Though Fanny was unable to obtain a college degree, she was a lifelong learner and committed to providing her own children and children less fortunate with as much education as possible. In Samuel Mag, Fanny found a partner who shared her values and was both educated and successful in business. The two established a home in New Britain, Connecticut, and Fanny worked off and on in the family clothing store. She had a strong sense of public service and social justice which led to

> Joan Karff's daughter, Rachel Karff Weissenstein, summarizes her mother's life lessons:
>
> 1. *Be kind to others. This means people in your family, as well as the waitress at the restaurant and the clerk at the grocery store.*
>
> 2. *Value ideas over things.*
>
> 3. *Read books...lots and lots of books. Watch the news. Be aware of the world you live in.*
>
> 4. *Find a life partner whom you respect and who respects you. Take care of each other every day. Some days will be 80-20 days and some will be 50-50. It will all even out in the end if you've chosen the right person.*
>
> 5. *Follow your passion. Find the thing that brings you joy and do it!*
>
> 6. *Be creative. Your imagination is one of your greatest gifts.*
>
> 7. *Don't be a drama queen or a troublemaker.*
>
> 8. *Move through the world with grace. Forgive others their flaws or indiscretions.*
>
> 9. *Find a way to pay it forward. Make someone else feel lucky for having known you. Reach out to those in need. Be a force for good in the world.*

Fanny Mittau

an active life in local politics. She also studied dance and piano as an adult and was learning new music until the day she died.

Fanny was a devoted mother to her three children. She was also conscious of the needs of less fortunate families; thus, she advocated for better schools and played a major role in the establishment of a dance program in Hartford's public school system. Fanny worked with Literacy Volunteers of America and the League of Women Voters and, in 1964, was elected to her district's Office of Economic Opportunity. She was the first woman, and the first Jew, to hold public office in the district of New Britain.

By all accounts, Samuel Mag was an ideal mate for the formidable Fanny Mittau. Educated, successful, and fun-loving, Samuel Mag came from a family whose rise from immigrant poverty was extraordinary, but hardly unprecedented. As Eastern European Jews, Samuel's parents were part of the largest wave of immigration by a single ethnic group in American history (1881–1914). Living under the oppressive rule of

Czarist Russia, the Mag sons would have faced early conscription into the Russian Army and an education would have been unlikely. These discriminatory policies toward Jews and the anti-Semitism that had plagued the region for centuries grew worse with the passage of the May Laws in 1881. Spurred by the darkening clouds over Eastern European Jewry, the Mags were among the thousands who arrived at Ellis Island

Fanny Mittau, Hartford, CT

Fanny Mittau Mag, mother of Joan, center in black

Biography of a Mentor

New Britain, CT, circa 1950

Fanny Mag with a friend

with empty pockets and a long surname. Neither remained for long. They became the Mags and the family leapt from abject poverty on Manhattan's Lower East Side to the leafy suburbs of Connecticut in a single generation. The family's clothing business grew from peddling to bricks and mortar and, in spite of quotas on Jewish students at the time, Samuel's parents were able to send him and several other male members of the family to Ivy League Yale University in New Haven, Connecticut.

Fanny and Samuel Mag had a happy marriage and by the time their second child, Joan, was born, the family business, Mag and Sons Co., was a successful men's clothing store in New Britain. Samuel and Fanny were married for forty years when he died in 1972. Fanny met and married her second husband, Victor Fassler, in 1979. She continued to be an active volunteer for various organizations, tutoring new immigrants, learning new music on the piano, and sharing her views until her death in 1994, at the age of eighty-seven.

FORMAL EDUCATION

Karff's mother made sure her own children had the academic opportunities and the exposure to culture that she had been raised to value but could not afford to enjoy herself. This meant that Joan saw every major dance company that came through Hartford. It also meant that literature and the arts were household priorities.

The Mags' commitment to learning was typical, but they were unusually broad-minded when it came to gender. They wanted both of their daughters as well as their son to receive the best education possible. The public school in New Britain was not particularly good and prompted Karff's older sister to start looking for an alternative. She discovered a boarding school for girls in western Massachusetts and convinced her parents to send her and Joan to the Northfield School for Girls.

The Northfield Seminary for Young Ladies (as it was then called) was located on the banks of the Connecticut River in the rolling foothills of the Berkshire Mountains. The school was founded by D. L. Moody, one of the best-known religious reformers of the nineteenth century, and a progressive thinker who set out to establish a boarding school for poor girls. Though Karff missed home and did not care for the school's restrictions governing interactions between girls and boys, she received an education that was a far cry from the finishing schools that would have been a more common choice for girls from similar socioeconomic backgrounds. Northfield was a place to begin, not a place to finish. The school emphasized the arts, required ten hours of manual labor a week, and made choir a mandatory activity and the Protestant Hymnal a required text. Northfield was also unusually diverse and Karff's best friend was an African-American girl. Northfield was as progressive as Karff's own parents and, like her mother, Northfield gave its students a healthy dose of the arts and community service. Northfield was founded by a leader whose sense of duty was tied to his faith, and though Moody's evangelical Christianity was different from the traditions of the Mag family, Karff also was driven by faith. Karff does not explicitly link her current work with students to her Jewish identity, but she does see her work in the community on behalf of others as a Jewish obligation.

MOUNT HOLYOKE COLLEGE

After graduating from Northfield in 1953, Karff headed only a few miles south to attend the nation's oldest and most prestigious college open to women at that time. Mount Holyoke College is a Seven Sisters School, and Karff thrived in this heady academic environment. Although Mount Holyoke did not offer a dance major, Joan spent more time in the dance studio than anywhere else, studying with modern dance pioneer Helen Priest Rogers.

> *Mount Holyoke College knew about educating women, but it took the activism of the 1960s and '70s to really give women access to higher and more meaningful roles of leadership in every field—medicine, law, the sciences, politics, etc.*
>
> —*Joan Karff*

Mount Holyoke College in the 1950's

Museum Visit, Mount Holyoke College, 1959

WOMEN ON THE WAY UP

Joan graduated magna cum laude and Phi Beta Kappa from Mount Holyoke in 1958. Even so, she was still uncertain about her future. She had been accepted to the school of social work at Simmons College in Boston, but had also applied for a job as a dance instructor at Hofstra College in Hempstead, New York. She ultimately chose Hofstra, spending a formative year there as a member of the dance faculty. When she headed to the Long Island, New York campus, she wasn't sure if dance would be a lifelong career, but she definitely was excited about the opportunity.

Graduation

MARRIAGE AND FAMILY

> *Mom was an always-there mom, even though she had this other creative dancing life. She was the tuck-you-into-bed and make-up-silly-stories mom and the drive-you-to-school and pack-your-lunch mom.*
>
> —Rachel Karff Weissenstein

Joan Mag met her future husband at a Shabbat service in Hartford, Connecticut. Samuel Karff was a handsome young Harvard-educated rabbi and Joan found his intellect and ambition appealing. Sam Karff, who grew up in Philadelphia, was both an athlete and scholar. After accelerating his studies at Harvard, he headed to Hebrew Union College in Cincinnati, Ohio where he was ordained. He spent two years as an Air Force chaplain, after which he accepted a position as an assistant rabbi at the

Miss Joan Mag, Holyoke Graduate, Engaged to Rabbi

Mr. and Mrs. Samuel E. Mag of New Britain announce the engagement of their daughter, Joan, to Rabbi Samuel E. Karff, son of Mr. and Mrs. Louis Karff of Philadelphia, Pa. The wedding is planned for June.

The bride-elect attended the Northfield, Mass. School for Girls and was graduated Magna Cum Laude from Mount Holyoke college, where she was elected to Phi Beta Kappa. She is a teacher of modern dance at Hofstra college, Hempstead, L. I.

Rabbi Karff, who is assistant rabbi of Temple Beth Israel in West Hartford, was graduated Magna Cum Laude from Harvard, and was ordained at Hebrew Union college in Cincinnati, Ohio. Also a member of Phi Beta Kappa, he served as an Air Force chaplain.

SAMUEL E. KARFF
222 Homer St.   Newton Centre, Mass.
BI 4-6716
1816 Lindley Ave.
Central High School
Softball, Touch Football, Writing, History, Government Economics, Political Clubs: American's Democratic Action.

Biography of a Mentor

Reform Synagogue in West Hartford, Connecticut, where he eventually met Joan. Sam and Joan spent their first year of marriage in West Hartford and then moved to Flint, Michigan for another two years. Sam was the senior rabbi there until 1962. They then settled in an affluent community of Chicago, where Sam became the senior rabbi of the historic Chicago Sinai Congregation. The couple had three daughters, and while tending to a growing family, Rabbi Karff also built a reputation as a scholar and pulpit rabbi. Though her primary focus was her family, Joan continued to study dance and was a dance instructor at the National College of Education in Chicago for seven years.

> *After fifty-six years of marriage, I can enthusiastically say I got it right the first time. It was extremely important to me to find a husband with whom I could share a love of ideas. An inquisitive mind and a kind heart were essential to my twenty-two-year-old self. So it was a combination of very good luck and the ability to recognize those characteristics in a man that led me to Sam Karff. It wasn't necessary that we share all the same interests. But it was important for me, as it is for everyone who seeks a good marriage, to find a partner who will grow with you, who will value the same things, and who will be deserving of respect as well as love.*
>
> *—Joan Karff*

In Chicago, Joan also crystallized her belief in the importance of arts instruction, especially dance. In an article entitled, "Dance and the Urban School," she articulates the value of dance instruction in public urban schools and defines dance as a "guided exploration into the world of movement by which young people learn to utilize their imagination."

The Karffs' three daughters describe their parents as a couple who support each other and make family their priority. Despite juggling the demands of their father's very public career, the Karffs built a strong, mutually supportive partnership. As their daughter, Amy Karff Halevy, puts it:

> *Mom and Dad both had fairly public images, but in different ways. When we were growing up, Dad's image seemed to be something that you were constantly reminded of—every time we went somewhere as a family, someone would approach Dad. He has always been incredible at remembering names (something Mom has a gift for as well).*

Dad never seemed bothered or annoyed at the intrusion. He knew that it was part of the job. Mom also had a very high tolerance and acceptance for this part of his life. I really attribute that to the fact that when they are alone together, they are really together. Their true love and devotion to each other is always evident. And while that could have made us feel left out, it never did. They just seemed to find the right balance of "Mommy and Daddy time" and family time and still do what they needed to do for their respective careers.

Samuel Karff and his three daughters

ACTIVISM

While their work differed, the Karffs built their life around shared values and priorities. They were devoted to each other and to their daughters, but both were concerned about social justice and leaned toward activism. Rabbi Karff was a point person on race relations during the turbulent 1960s, and Joan became involved in the bitterly divided public school system by teaching and writing about the value of art—especially dance—in schools.

> *We compensated for the highly public social dimension to our lives by taking a two-month working sabbatical in Charlevoix, Michigan each summer. I would spend six mornings a week in study and writing, and Joan would choreograph for her dance company. When our daughters were young enough to be with us, we generally declined all evening social engagements that might take us away from them. They all have wonderful memories of summers in Charlevoix.*
>
> —*Rabbi Samuel Karff*

The Karff family moved to Houston in 1975. At that time, their daughters were fourteen, thirteen, and ten. Rabbi Karff became the senior rabbi of Congregation Beth Israel and, as their children got older, Joan was able to devote herself to dance. She was on the faculty of Rice University. In 1976, she formed a professional modern dance company, the New Dance Group. The ensemble was the Houston Jewish Community Center's resident company for twenty-five years. Joan ran every aspect of the company, including the creation of thirty-five new works.

During the course of her tenure with the New Dance Group, Joan worked with the Houston Independent School District (HISD) to offer a series of performances in the local schools. It was a positive experience and she felt that a school would be the ideal backdrop for the next stage of her life's work. While she had been in and around public schools in Houston, Chicago, and New York, these interactions had taken place through dance. In 2000, as she prepared to disband the company, she approached her longtime friend and former HISD superintendent Ray Reiner and shared with him her idea of forming a mentoring group in a public school for high-school-age girls.

Joan Karff (center) is surrounded by members of her New Dance Group: G. Carlos Henderson, Kerry Wright, Erica Wyckoff, Sarah Barry, Macarena Ortuzar and Stacey Shively.

AN IDEA BECOMES A REALITY

Ray Reiner previously had served as principal of two HISD middle schools before serving as principal of Lamar High School from 1984 to 1988. Since Reiner and Karff's friendship went back twenty-five years, Reiner knew Karff's strengths and was certain she would be a tremendous asset in the right context. Given the population and administration

Biography of a Mentor

of Lamar, Reiner felt that Lamar would be an ideal setting for WOWU.

Since its inception in 2001, Karff personally has seen 150 young women graduate from WOWU. The graduates go on to attend institutions of higher learning and pursue ambitious dreams that perhaps did not seem to be within their reach prior to their participation in WOWU. Because of the program's unique curriculum and use of community resources, such as leading professionals and cultural offerings, WOWU participants are introduced to a world they may not otherwise have seen. After graduation, the women return year after year to share what life has been like for them since high school. As the family of WOWU graduates expands, the network of resources available to current WOWU participants continues to grow and multiply.

Karff's own life is a rich tapestry of experiences that stretches across many fields of study. She has integrated these professional experiences with her familial role and created a life in which her multiple roles do not compete, but rather enhance one another. She shares her story when it is appropriate, but she focuses WOWU group discussions on the human being who composed the music or wrote the book being discussed that week. Whether it is art, literature, or a guest speaker, she is always intent on highlighting the factors that led to the creation of the work of art or the career path of the person in front of the young women.

While Karff cares deeply about WOWU participants, giving each one her personal attention, she does not approach them with a preconceived notion of how or what will motivate them. She delights in the unexpected insights that come from dialogue, whether spoken aloud, written, or, in the case of dance, physical. Perhaps this is why the meticulous and relatively subdued Karff allows her students to write on the walls of a room in her house at the end-of-the-year gathering. She literally hands them a permanent marker and says, "Draw or write whatever you want on these walls." It is not surprising that they scribble accolades and words of thanks.

WOMEN ON THE WAY UP

4A
Thursday, June 23, 2011
bellaireeditor@hcnonline.com
www.YourBellaireNews.com

VIEW

Mentoring program leads gi

STEVE MARK
On the Mark

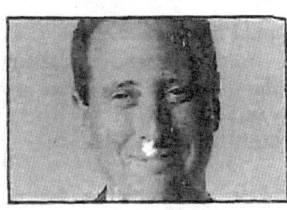

Ten years ago, Evelyn Rico-Soto was entering her senior year at Lamar High School, somewhat spirited about her post-high school future but unsure of her college path. Veterinary medicine seemed a reputable and safe choice.

Out of nowhere, coincidentally, came a mentor who helped Rico-Soto with the confidence to leap to a riskier, though more rewarding path.

Joan Karff, a longtime local dance instructor and founder of the New Dance Group, was looking for way to help students who wouldn't ordinarily have exposure to dance and the arts. She found immediate interest from the administration at Lamar, and quickly established Women On The Way Up, a group which includes 10 seniors each year. Members were selected with the following criteria: each student had to have some degree of interest in the arts, and had to be a product of a low-income background.

"I had raised daughters of my own, and wanted to give something back to the community," says Karff, who previously conducted many lecture demos at HISD schools.

Just the timing Evelyn Rico-Soto needed. She was selected to Karff's first group of seniors who spent part of every Thursday afternoon together, attending seminars on careers, parenting and public speaking. Trips to the Houston Symphony and Houston Ballet became part of the annual schedule. Karff's underlying theme was a constant awareness of current events.

"She really gave us the tools to be independent," says Evelyn, who calls herself one of the "pioneer girls" of the program and is now a financial counselor for Memorial Hermann Northwest. "She exposed us to new aspects of what we had to be prepared for-how to budget, and things to expect later in life, like balancing families and careers."

Prior to each year Karff interviews between 30-35 girls for the program. "I ask them all kinds of questions, but what I am really interested in is if there is any spark of intellectual curiosity. Do you really want to explore your world? When I touch that little spark, that's when I know they are right for the program."

"Mostly they are just eager to do better than their parents have done, and to make their mark in the world," adds Karff. "They are great examples of success."

Inclusion in the club also means a $1,000 scholarship each student. Karff's ongoing efforts mean she's raised

Biography of a Mentor

OINTS

to become strong women

Photo by STEVE MARK/For the Examiner

...omen On The Way Up participants surrounding program founder Joan Karff.

100,000 since the creation of Women On The Way Up. Foundations and private donors assist with the scholarship funding.

"A lot of us were minority women, and the first in our families to go to college," says ...ico-Soto, who attended the University of Houston and majored in theater. "It was really great for someone to give us the opportunity."

Every year the club has a reunion, meaning the upcoming guest list now numbers 100. Aside from catching up on career and family, Women On The Way Up benefits from some effective in-house networking.

"So many of them are inspirational," says Karff.

And in this case, Karff's greatest step teaching has little to do with those on the dance floor.

Women on the way Up

CHAPTER TWO

HOW AND WHY WOMEN ON THE WAY UP WORKS

> *Underserved students are defined as students who do not receive equitable resources as other students in the academic pipeline. Typically, these groups of students include low-income, under-represented racial/ethnic minorities and first-generation students, as well as many others.*
>
> —***National Inventory of Academic Pathways***

Joan Karff's proposal of mentoring underserved females was modest in size and limited in scope, but she knew that it would be most effective if she could find a school administration willing to collaborate and offer some of its resources. Ray Reiner knew that Lamar principal Dr. James McSwain would appreciate the value of what Karff had to offer, and he was correct. McSwain's own life experience is proof of that. Raised in a family of modest means with parents who were not college graduates, McSwain insists that he never would have made it to college himself had it not been for a teacher who took an interest in him and helped him research schools and fill out college applications. He says that believing in him literally raised him up.

McSwain's and Lamar High School's active support of Karff and WOWU were invaluable.

> *I valued education and saw it as the pathway of success. Lamar is a very heterogeneous school and I wanted to mentor young women who were financially disadvantaged and a member of a minority group. I wanted to present the wonderful world of culture and literature to them and at the same time reward them by offering a scholarship.*
>
> —*Joan Karff*

Initially, parents of WOWU students sometimes hesitated to send their daughters off campus on a Sunday field trip with a woman who was not employed or paid by the school. But the school administration's explicit support of Karff reassured parents and was especially important in the program's early years. The school has provided space and logistical support by allowing the school district's fine arts coordinator, Dr. Gary Patterson, to work with the program. Patterson makes sure that WOWU participants do not have scheduling conflicts since the gatherings take place during school hours. Patterson also assists in the selection process, administers the scholarship funds, and coordinates the logistics for the field trips.

HOW AND WHY EACH STUDENT IS CHOSEN

WOWU engages each student on a very personal level, which is reflected by the selection process. This process begins in the students' junior year. The Lamar administration selects a group of thirty to forty highly motivated young women who are good students, come from underserved backgrounds, and have expressed an interest in going to college. These students are invited to apply by written essays that are reviewed by Karff. Based on these essays, Karff invites students to one-on-one interviews. She eventually narrows the group

WOWU grads with certificates of completion

down to ten participants, and they begin meeting in the fall of their senior year for an hour and a half on Thursday afternoons. At the end of the school year, each student receives $1,000 to be used toward college tuition.

Though Karff does not have a narrow view of success, one of her only absolute requirements for acceptance is the student's desire to attend college. While skills and test scores are important, they do not always lead to a degree, or to a career, if acquired by a person who does not believe in herself or lacks a desire to learn. The desire to attend college indicates a level of willingness to achieve at whatever the student feels called to pursue, and Karff believes that a college degree is a credential that will give the "Women on the Way Up" many options. Karff does not have a fixed notion about whom students should become, nor how they will get there. As an artist, she is most interested in their journey and she offers them key tools in order to navigate this journey. She encourages the young women to be curious and hardworking, and then introduces them to a range of people, ideas, and experiences that develop their thinking about the world.

A UNIQUE FUNDING STRATEGY

WOWU has not had to focus its fund-raising on an operating budget or accumulation of capital funds because Lamar High School has covered a range of small, but necessary, administrative costs. In addition, because the program is small, Lamar also has been able to underwrite the cost of field trip tickets and transportation through its allocated arts programming funds. As a result, Karff has not had to spend an inordinate amount of time fund-raising, which has freed her up to spend the bulk of her time running the program and developing relationships with the students.

Karff's main financial responsibility is raising $10,000 each year, enough to give each participant a $1,000 college scholarship upon completion of the program. Raising this amount each year has its benefits. Programs that do not require any financial support from the community often go unnoticed and underappreciated, while a small amount of fund-raising becomes a way to gain partners. Since the average contribution to the scholarship fund is relatively small, there is a long list of individuals outside of the school who know about and support WOWU. Most of the donors would not otherwise have been aware of the program's young women, but through the supportive relationship encouraged by the program, WOWU helps connect community members to each other.

This small but significant contribution has also shown WOWU participants that there is a community beyond the school that believes in them and is willing to support them. Further, the fund-raising effort raises awareness about the challenges faced by underserved students, the schools that serve them, and the success they can achieve with the support of programs like WOWU. This type of program cannot—and should not—stand on its own; the history of WOWU shows there is more to be gained by working in cooperation with public education institutions and outside supporters from the community.

PROGRAM CONTENT AND METHODS

On an afternoon in mid-March, ten female Lamar High School seniors are preparing for an upcoming trip to the Houston Ballet. Karff delivers a summary of the history of dance and then asks the students to do a few brief exercises to illustrate this history. She leans on the stereo speaker as she describes the reasons and motions of a rain dance. Then she asks them to form two lines before teaching them a few components of a partnered dance style associated with the royal courts of Renaissance Europe. Karff also takes the class through the positions of classical ballet showing them how the arms and feet are set for each position, from first through fifth. There are peals of laughter and some shouting as school lets out and an ocean of students spills out onto the courtyard directly below this dance lesson, but all ten sets of eyes remain on Karff.

Karff asks one student, who happens to have a background in dance, to demonstrate a step that is synonymous with Martha Graham and the boundary-breaking objectives of modern dance. The WOWU participant is a tall, slim, African-American student who looks particularly young, wears glasses, and has her hair pulled back. She downplays her long and slender frame in her school sweatshirt and mismatched scarf. After a few instructions from Karff, she moves to one end of the room and proceeds to execute the exaggerated step that looks like a slow-motion run. "Now, do that again, but look here, and then here and then here," Karff suggests. She listens, returns to the corner, and then proceeds to glide across the room in a few brilliant, long motions. She is all arms and legs. She's breathtaking. Her classmates are still and focused on her, despite the shouts of students from the courtyard below. Karff watches and smiles broadly. "Yes, beautiful. Exactly like that."

WOWU's content and methods are intended to help students develop the intellectual and personal maturity necessary for future success. It is a yearlong program that facilitates the social, emotional, and intellectual growth of female students by expanding their worldview and challenging them to examine their assumptions. Toward this end, they visit Houston's premier cultural institutions, guided by local leaders in the arts. They meet with minority women who have become successful in various professions. They deliver oral reports on outstanding women, each one selected by Karff based on what she knows about each student. They discuss personal issues from teen pregnancy to financial responsibility, along with world events and politics. For many, this is the first time they have participated in conversations about controversial or topical events. Karff is a nonjudgmental guide with high expectations. She establishes clear parameters for what will be discussed at each gathering by offering a predictable format filled with interesting and sometimes surprising content. It is a format that ignites their interest and then encourages them to share ideas or questions that arise.

WOWU AND THE ARTS

One year, during a field trip to a Houston Symphony Orchestra concert, Dr. Patterson (who holds a doctorate in choral music) gathers the WOWU students in the lobby during intermission. He calls attention to various aspects of the performance that relate to topics the group had discussed earlier. Patterson has a rare ability to explain fairly abstract musical concepts clearly, conveying a compelling reverence for the music. Listening to Patterson give a lecture on musicology, one realizes that a reason the arts have become so integral to this program is there has been an exceptionally gifted arts educator working alongside Karff.

The students attend a matinee performance, hearing a program that includes Mendelssohn's *Octet for Strings in E Flat Major*. Not a single one of the young women has ever been to the symphony

WOWU at ballet performance

before, and yet, the moment the last bars are played, the young women leap to their feet without pause and join in a well-deserved standing ovation. Their genuine appreciation is a reflection of how seamlessly WOWU incorporates the arts into its curriculum. The week prior, Dr. Patterson spends a Thursday afternoon preparing the young ladies for what they are going to be hearing, and after the performance they go to dinner at a lovely restaurant and discuss the performance they just heard. These are purposeful choices.

WOWU aims to do more than merely expose students to the arts. WOWU creates a set of circumstances that gives students the opportunity to fall in love with the symphony, ballet, literature, and art museums. Students from lower socioeconomic environments often do not have the opportunity to be exposed to these cultural institutions, and they certainly do not often find themselves in settings where the arts are experienced and discussed with the regularity that Karff was fortunate enough to experience in her life. She has always been involved in the arts, and WOWU's content is informed by her experiences.

While there are ample studies that reflect the positive impact of the study of music, dance, and visual arts on the evolving intellect of young people, WOWU demonstrates that the arts also help students develop a level of appreciation for creativity. The arts programming also appeals to the young women's emotions in a way that other content does not. In the company of truly outstanding artists and arts educators like Karff and Patterson, WOWU members are given an opportunity to see the meaning and purpose that human beings find in the arts. With relatively little preparation, the members of WOWU are able to appreciate even fairly abstract works of art and obscure musical compositions. In general, WOWU is not simply about exposing students to specific works of art, compositions, or performances. Instead, these interactions with art and artists are meant to give them the opportunity to appreciate the universal truths about human potential and creativity that are revealed by the art they witness or hear.

The young women are also asked to reflect on their experiences. Karff asks them to write in their journals after field trips, a process that facilitates their intellectual development. These revelations shift the internal landscape of the participants. After visiting an Impressionism exhibit at the Museum of Fine Arts in Houston, a student writes, "Seeing art is like taking a trip through the artist's mind."

LITERATURE

If you did not know that Karff was a dancer and choreographer, you might assume she is a novelist or literature professor. Literature has been a constant in Karff's life, and she actively and consistently weaves her love of reading into everyday conversation. She enlisted the help of her daughter, Rachel Karff Weissenstein, an English teacher, in formulating a reading list for WOWU participants. The objective is not merely to introduce students to worthy authors and their work, but also to expand their awareness of the world by considering it through another's eyes.

Although Karff is well-read, she is not a literary snob. Literature serves as a passport to new ideas and cultures, and Karff approaches the different variations without judgment. She chooses books that will speak directly to her students, hoping to ignite a love of reading and a deeper awareness of the human experience. Rather than having each student read the same books at the same time, she assigns each one a different book about a woman whose life relates in some way to the reader. Students then report to the class on what they have read. This method gives each participant a chance to bring something to the group that no one else can offer. It is a subtle and effective way of developing a community of learners, rather than a group of acolytes.

Some of the books that Karff has included in the WOWU syllabus include *Kaffir Boy*, by Mark Mathabane; *The Kite Runner*, by Khaled Hosseini; and *Left to Tell*, by Immaculée Ilibagiza. A more complete list can be found in this book's appendix.

> *Books were a big part of our lives growing up. I quickly learned that books did not really count as material possessions in the same way as say, a set of electric rollers might; I understood that books were sort of magical vessels containing stories and ideas and knowledge and imagination. I was a writer from a very young age and my stories and poems and song lyrics were always marveled at and appreciated. No big surprise then that I became an English teacher.*
>
> —*Rachel Karff Weissenstein*

> *And I understood that the gift of the blessing of being able to think in a wide-ranging fashion and amid a multiplicity of connections, that this magnificent ability, the only true way to contemplate the world from a multiplicity of vantage points at once, is only granted to the man who transcends his own experience to absorb from books what they can tell of many lands and peoples and times.*
>
> —*Stefan Zweig*
> ***German author***

CURRENT EVENTS

Karff wants her students to be aware of the world they will be entering as adults and includes current events in WOWU programming. The group discussions are aimed at broadening their understanding of the world. This can be a challenging process, and conversations within the safety of WOWU give participants tolerance for opposing views and a perspective that strengthens their ability to interpret the world. Karff raised her own daughters to be aware of themselves and the world around them. She seeks the same level of conversation from the WOWU group that she would of her own daughters, and somehow the students know that this comes from her faith in their abilities and a desire to see them succeed. Daughter Amy recalls riding in the car with her mother listening to the radio during the resignation of President Nixon: "She turned to Rachel and me and said, 'Listen, girls—this is history.'"

ROLE MODELS

Karff is just one of many individuals with whom the young women interact during the course of the yearlong experience. She establishes herself as a guide and connector, rather than an expert on everything. Karff creates a framework for learning and discussion and then brings an array of individuals with varying areas of expertise into the group.

WOWU reunion at Karff home

As a result, students not only learn from these guests, but they also have the opportunity to observe the interactions that occur between adults who have achieved a level of success and knowledge in their chosen fields. The community of learners and professionals that Karff assembles becomes a statement to these students about their own potential. They begin to see that there are people who have overcome similar obstacles.

Though Karff is white and Jewish, most WOWU participants are not of the same faith, and most are women of color. They do not necessarily identify with her, but they do trust her. Knowing that she does not share her students' background, she seeks successful minority women to serve as guest speakers and fellow mentors. She pays close attention to the details that students share about their lives and tinkers with the syllabus every year to include specific content that will address an area of interest, or a specific student's challenge. She invites particular speakers because they can offer information about the careers her students have expressed an interest in pursuing. This also applies to aspects of her own life, which she shares when it relates to the choices and challenges that young women on the cusp of adulthood are likely to face. As a result, Karff's students feel that she hears and understands them, and they demonstrate an eagerness to see the world through her eyes.

Furthermore, the WOWU participants gain confidence by observing that an impressive array of individuals take the time to be with them and that they do so with great enthusiasm. By inviting upstanding women to visit with the group, Karff conveys to the students that she is confident in their abilities. As one graduate put it, "These were very smart, successful, and busy women. It dawned on me one day that if this person was taking the time to be with us, then we must be up to the task."

Karff focuses the discussions with visitors on the importance of asking the right questions, rather than giving all the right answers. In a small group of only women, Karff is able to model and encourage students to be inquisitive. Asking for help becomes a sign of intelligence and maturity rather than a weakness. Having an all-female group increases the likelihood of candid exchanges between students and role models, and these conversations help the students make informed choices about their future education and their lives.

COMMUNITY

The fact that nearly every participant in the program has graduated from college affirms the efficacy of mentoring for underserved students. Mentoring seems to allow underserved (and often minority) students to take advantage of the initiatives and programs intended to help increase college matriculation.

Members of WOWU obtain scholarships, benefit from affirmative action, and find supplemental academic help and testing preparation, if necessary. All of these factors undoubtedly play a role in the near-perfect record of college graduation for WOWU participants. Mentoring seems to ground these students and help them to navigate the labyrinth of support that exists, but is not always found, by its targeted audience. For the young participants in WOWU, Karff has been the bridge between female students who may have had limited prospects, given their circumstances and a lack of needed personal attention, and a universe of ideas and people who can help them. The network provided by WOWU includes school officials, successful local women, and graduates of the program.

There is a mutually beneficial relationship between Lamar High School and WOWU. Lamar's faculty and administration are aware of the less-than-favorable odds faced by some of their students. Lamar is one of the oldest and one of the largest high schools in the fourth largest city in the United States. The Houston Independent School District (HISD) has had its share of criticism, but it has demonstrated an impressive commitment to the well-being of its students by supporting WOWU, even though it is a small program run by an outsider. Understanding the value of publicly acknowledging success stories, Lamar demonstrates its pride in the students of WOWU by allowing the organization and its graduates to be publicly recognized on graduation day. Reiner describes the power of these moments:

> *When that young lady walks across the stage to receive her diploma, she is going somewhere. You hear 'Women on the Way Up,' and people know it; the school takes great pride in these girls, and they should. Each one will be successful. You can be sure of it.*

WOMEN ON THE WAY UP

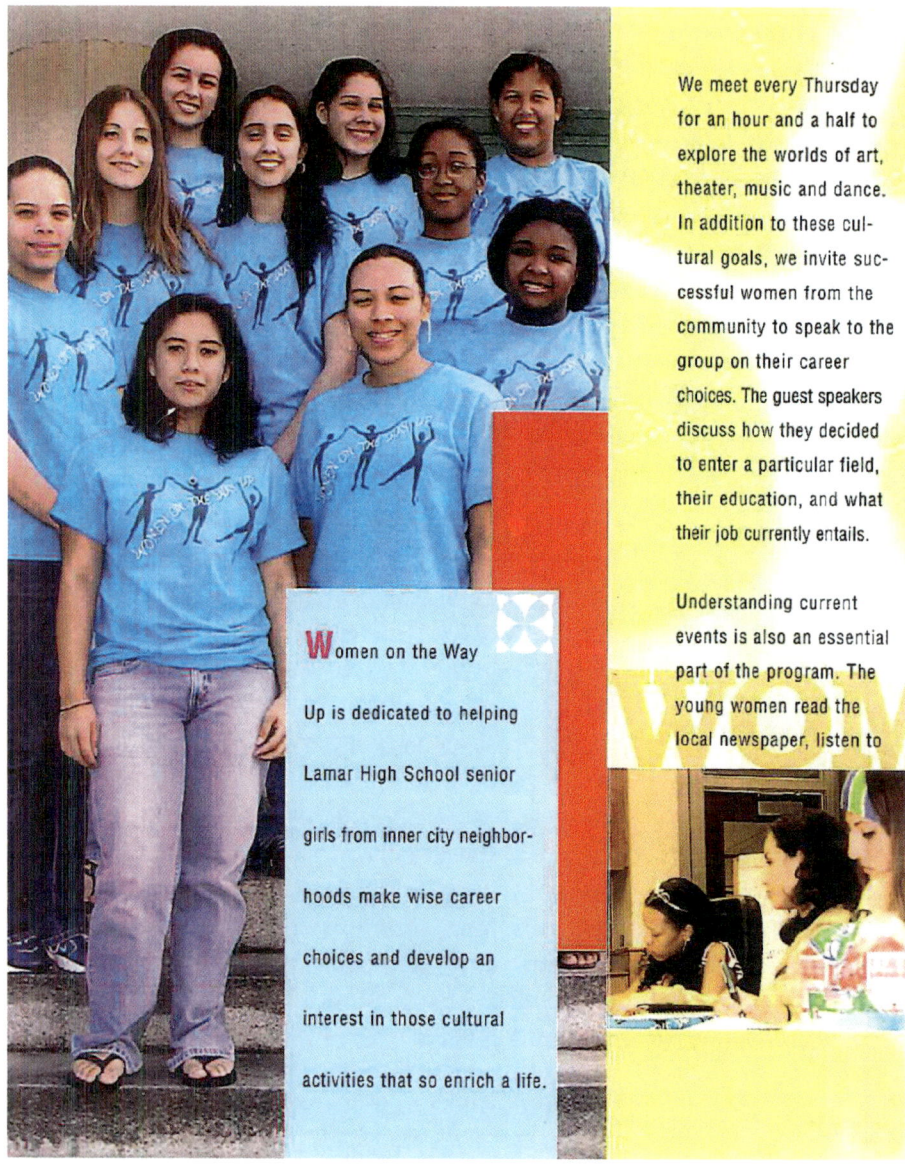

Women on the Way Up is dedicated to helping Lamar High School senior girls from inner city neighborhoods make wise career choices and develop an interest in those cultural activities that so enrich a life.

We meet every Thursday for an hour and a half to explore the worlds of art, theater, music and dance. In addition to these cultural goals, we invite successful women from the community to speak to the group on their career choices. The guest speakers discuss how they decided to enter a particular field, their education, and what their job currently entails.

Understanding current events is also an essential part of the program. The young women read the local newspaper, listen to

How and Why Women on the Way Up Works

Joan Karff,
Director

At the completion of the program, each girl receives a $1,000 scholarship, directed to the college or university of her choice.

Tax-deductible contributions from the community are encouraged. Please mail your gift to:

Women on the Way Up
C/O Dr. James McSwain, Principal
Lamar High School
3325 Westheimer
Houston, TX 77098

news reports on TV, and research the internet, New York Times, and Wall Street Journal for a fuller awareness of world affairs.

Personal topics such as managing relationships, handling money, and obtaining the right skills to be a parent are discussed.

*Women
on the way
Up*

CHAPTER THREE

WOWU'S PLACE IN EDUCATION

On the second floor of Lamar High School, there is a boardroom lined with glass display cases, filled with items that represent the school's lengthy and storied past. There is a long conference table surrounded by wide, plush chairs, and on sunny days the light streams in through a bank of windows above the main entrance of the school. Clearly, this space is not intended to be a classroom. It has a definite VIP ambiance, and the school uses it for important meetings with the board, faculty, and other supporters. Every Thursday the ten members of WOWU—girls who are mostly African-American or Latina, and who seem especially small and young sitting in these oversize office chairs—gather here with Karff and occupy these seats of empowerment.

LAMAR HIGH SCHOOL

Built during the Great Depression, Lamar High is one of the largest public high schools in the Houston Independent School District, with 3,350 students. Lamar serves a remarkably diverse student body: approximately 36 percent Hispanic, 29 percent African-American, 28 percent Caucasian, and 7 percent Asian and other races. Over 47 percent of the students enrolled at Lamar are economically disadvantaged. The school also serves students residing at seven different homeless shelters within its attendance zone.

While WOWU came to reside at Lamar for logistical and circumstantial reasons, the school's community focus makes it an ideal home for the program. As an International Baccalaureate (IB) school, Lamar is consciously and consistently connected to its locale, and WOWU fits comfortably into this philosophy of community-oriented education.

From the moment they are selected for the group until the day they receive their high school diplomas, WOWU participants are treated as success stories. They are expected to show up, work hard, and contribute; there is no question that Karff and the school have high expectations for these students. But by being chosen as a member of WOWU, these young women have been told in no uncertain terms that they are capable of reaching high standards. These intellectual and interpersonal expectations are evidence of the tremendous faith that their mentor and the school have in each one of them. Through Karff, the school conveys its confidence and, by virtue of their hard work and dedication, these young women rekindle the community's faith in education and its important role in empowering youth.

FOCUSING ON EFFECTIVE GUIDANCE

Programs designed to help underserved students often do so by responding to the specific deficits they face, economics being a major factor. While Karff knows that one cannot mend society alone, she believes that each of her students has the capacity to overcome familial, economic, and personal challenges. Thus, the program is not only intended to offer some of the information and skills that will aid these students in the future, but it is also intended to convince them that they can achieve their goals. In short, Karff recognizes the challenges faced by her mentees, but she chooses instead to focus on their potential. Community mentoring programs like WOWU seem to harness the optimism of the individuals and institutions involved.

Education is still a reliable way for an individual to break the cycle of poverty, but the matriculation patterns for minority and underserved students are not easily changed. For underserved students, making college possible is not the same as making it probable. Obtaining a degree is the final step in a lengthy process that most students—and parents—need help navigating. Most underserved high school students are not clear on how to manage the information-gathering, application, and selection process of applying to college, let alone how to accurately assess the various educational and financial options that come with successfully moving from high school to college. Studies on the impact of programs meant to increase enrollment among minorities have shown that without assistance, most minority high school students will not diverge from the established educational patterns of their peer group—regardless of their academic credentials.

Even if a student manages to perform well academically, good grades and test scores alone are not enough to unlock the doors of higher education. Students need guidance, and schools need aid in order to provide that guidance. For underserved students, the biggest obstacle is the belief that their problems are too extensive and that they are already too far behind to have a chance at success. Mentoring programs like WOWU have the potential to use the greatest resource that any community has to help these students achieve success—the experience of successful community members.

MENTORSHIP AND THE SMALL GROUP MODEL

Evelyn Rico Soto, Yeiry Guevara, Joan, Ahna Ramos, and Ashley Brantley get together

There is no single model for a mentoring program that would work in all schools, but a thoughtful and concerted effort to utilize interested and qualified members of the community as mentors in overburdened public schools is an idea well worth exploring. It is clear that meeting this need—even if only for a handful of students—does not require extensive funding in order to have a positive impact. Mentoring programs build a bridge of support between a community and its next generation of professionals.

At the core of all mentoring relationships is the student's desire to be heard by her mentor. In a sense, there is no mentoring relationship without this need and certainly no effective mentoring relationship without a mentor who understands and is worthy of her role. On most days that the group meets, WOWU students do not need to be prodded to contribute, nor do they need to be silenced when their mentor, Karff, speaks. Sometimes she shares her own life experience, and at other times she brings an individual from the community, whose life becomes the topic of conversation. Books, cultural experiences, and current events are also subjects that provide the content of WOWU. Through these topics, the students are challenged to think about their own path. They accept this challenge because they trust Karff. Though she does not share their background, through the topics she chooses and the guests she invites, they see that she understands and supports them. It is a different model from a one-on-one mentoring relationship, but it is more consistent with Karff's educational background and her experience in working with groups as a choreographer and dance instructor.

In a small group, students learn not only by interacting with each other; they also learn by observing the interactions of others. The group model provides an opportunity to practice the kind of group discussion that students in large classrooms may not have the opportunity to experience. Many underserved students are expected to learn in large classrooms in which small group discussion is uncommon. Furthermore, many students who are from lower-income backgrounds have succeeded in doing well in large public schools because they have not been the proverbial "squeaky wheel." They often fly under the radar and do not cause too much of a stir. The obedience that helped these young women do well in lower grades, however, does not always serve them well in later years, when success requires them to be vocal and advocate for themselves.

The later years of education are not a new type of challenge merely because they require students to be vocal. The last years of grade school and the subsequent years of higher education also require students to be self-reflective in a way that is often both foreign and difficult for students from families without ample resources. The college application process involves interviews and personal essays in which schools look for a coherent personal narrative. College-level learning often involves small group discussion that can be challenging for all students, but is especially so for underserved students who have been accustomed to getting by without making too much noise. WOWU is a small universe in which these young, often minority, women can begin to hear their own voices.

Women on the Way Up

Joan with babies Rachel and Amy
(Jan. 1962)

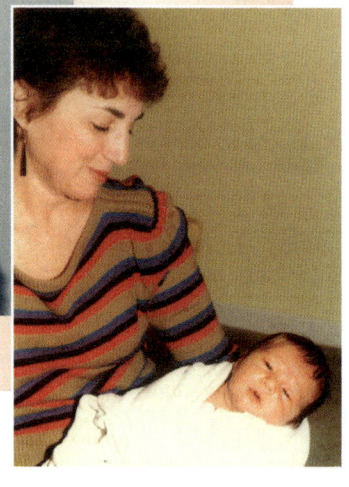

Grandma Joan and Joshua
Louis Weissenstein (Dec. 1985)

Joan & Daughter Liz
(Nov. 1974)

Joan with Meggi Seitz

CHAPTER FOUR

THE LEGACY OF AN UNCOMMON WOMAN

In mentoring young women, Joan Karff has managed to remain connected to her own mother—not only because she is doing something of which her mother would have approved, but because she must constantly recall and reiterate the reasons why the arts, literature, and learning in general are so essential. She is orchestrating WOWU during a stage of life when she is not constrained by the need to earn a living or raise young children—a time when she could have chosen to disconnect from the larger community and focus on her own family and interests.

On one level, this extraordinary effort is the mark of a person who is truly generous and community-oriented, but on another, it is the mark of an individual who lives a purpose-driven life. WOWU is the continuation of a life that has always been guided by a love of humanity in all of its spectacular variety. It also champions a love of learning for its own sake. Karff has twice battled cancer while running WOWU, but she never has left the program in someone else's hands. That is because running WOWU has been her way of remaining connected to the ideas that have defined her and given her strength.

In 1957, when Karff was a senior at Mount Holyoke College, the school's new president, Richard Glenn Gettell, gave an inaugural address entitled, "A Plea for the Uncommon Woman." The speech is an eloquent defense of education for women, a subject that was still hotly debated at the time. Gettell was responding to those who had cautioned that there were too few jobs in the American workforce to support the aspirations of an increased number of college graduates.

In his speech, Gettell argues that the kind of learning which leads to a liberal arts degree is especially critical for women—not because it will prepare them for a specific job, but because it will prepare them for a life in which they will be able to make a contribution, whether they are in the workforce, raising children, both, or beyond both of those phases in life. Gettell reasons that this enlightened and rigorous education cultivates individuals capable of being contributors in every phase of life and in many different circumstances:

> *For the uncommon woman, the woman of high intelligence and ability, who constitutes a great national reservoir of talent, we need to provide the training and help develop the motivation, so that society can benefit from her talent more fully.*

Karff was months away from graduating when that speech was delivered. She realized then that she was well on her way toward making a contribution in her world because she had had the good fortune of receiving this enlightened education.

WOWU students have the chance to observe and learn from several leading women who genuinely love learning and believe in its power to transform individuals. They are exposed to women who have found vocations, not merely jobs. But WOWU is hardly a series of career counseling sessions; rather, it is a program that encourages self-discovery as much as intellectual development. WOWU is not a direct response to the challenges of underserved young women. Instead, WOWU helps these students to cultivate a sense of themselves and the world around them, making it possible for them to find their place in the world. The program kindles a love of learning and shows them the rewards of learning for its own sake. This awakening is the key ingredient.

WOWU on a field trip

It is the confidence and optimism that these students derive from their participation in WOWU that make them effective advocates for themselves long after they graduate. In only nine months of Thursday-afternoon meetings and a handful of Saturday field trips, WOWU leaves a lifetime impact on its participants. Ten girls every year for fifteen years is remarkable, but the ongoing impact that this handful of students continues to have is endless. Their success should renew faith in the possibilities created by mentoring, by schools that are willing to collaborate, and by uncommon women like Joan Karff.

ALUMNAE PROFILES

Please note that some of the profiles on the following pages are incomplete, as there has not been contact with a few of the alumnae for several years. The current biographies we do have, however, indicate an amazing dedication to education and career in a wide range of fields and are a testament to the empowering nature and success of the WOWU program.

Enthusiastic
WOWU alumnae

CHAPTER FIVE

ALUMNAE PROFILES

Guadalupe Bravo-Perez
University of Houston

Roxanne (Fernandez) Aranda
San Jacinto College
University of Houston—
Downtown

Eboni Nicole Graham
Texas A&M University
Texas Southern University
American University of Paris

Pascale Jackson-Ouedraogo
University of Alaska

Brittany LlaShay Kelley
Prairie View A&M University
University of Phoenix

Raquel Lopez
University of Houston—
Downtown

Claudia Veronica Martir
University of Houston—
Downtown

Aarica N. McIntyre
Art Institute of Houston

Brionne Q. Mills
Texas Southern University
Lamar University
Rice University

Evelyn Rico-Soto
University of Houston
DeVry University

Women on the Way Up

Guadalupe Bravo-Perez, SHRM-CP graduated from the University of Houston in 2006 with a degree in psychology and is a certified HR professional. Guadalupe married shortly after graduating from college, and she and her husband have two children. In her spare time, she enjoys volunteering in the community and spending time with her family.

> *I am very grateful for the opportunities given to me through this program and cherish all the wonderful memories.*
>
> *—Guadalupe Bravo-Perez*

Roxanne Marie (Fernandez) Aranda always dreamed of becoming an accountant/CPA and began working for a CPA firm while attending Lamar High School. She received her associate degree from San Jacinto College and attended the University of Houston—Downtown. Roxanne is currently an accountant for a law firm in downtown Houston and is married with two young daughters.

> *I am very thankful and happy to have the career that I have and I am grateful for my wonderful husband and lovely daughters. I am focusing my time and energy on my girls with the hope that they will be wiser and stronger than I am when they are older. I am steps away from my dream career and have worked hard to achieve my dream salary. I have a beautiful, strong, and healthy family, and so, in the end, I am one happy woman! I am truly blessed and thankful!*
>
> *Joan, you are an amazing woman! Thank you for all that you do to encourage young women. Many thanks for allowing me to be a part of this.*
>
> *—Roxanne Marie (Fernandez) Aranda*

Eboni Nicole Graham graduated from Texas A&M University in December 2006 with a bachelor of arts degree in English. She continued her studies at Texas Southern University where she graduated with a master of arts degree in journalism in May 2010. Eboni then moved to Amarillo and

Alumnae Profiles: 2002, Year One

worked as a reporter for Amarillo Globe-News. In August 2015, she relocated to Paris, France to attend the American University of Paris to study global communication and launch her international journalism career.

Pascale Jackson-Ouedraogo continued her studies at the University of Alaska, where she earned a BA in anthropology. She enjoys her current job nurturing students as a middle school language arts teacher in the Spring Branch neighborhood of Houston and plans to continue as a teacher with a focus on museum education. Pascale is married with two children. She is also an active patron of the arts.

I was particularly affected by the 'A Day in the Life' series . . . it drove home whether I could personally relate to the profession.
—Pascale Jackson-Ouedraogo

Brittany LlaShay Kelley graduated from Prairie View A&M in 2007 with a BS in mechanical engineering and from the University of Phoenix in 2012 with a masters in business administration. She is currently employed by Boeing in Phoenix and hopes to start her own business one day.

Brionne Mills, a native Houstonian, received all of her primary and secondary education in Houston area public schools. This educational experience allowed her to see the wide economic disparities that are pervasive within Houston area school districts. It has been a great motivator for her to become a leader in the Houston system to make changes for students of the future. She believes the greatest impact can be in her hometown where she can understand on a personal level the obstacles and challenges that many students face.

Brionne began college at Texas Southern University in the Frederick Douglass Honors Program on an academic scholarship. The family-like environment provided a setting that was conducive to excelling academically. Here she was taught that while every student is capable of learning, one does so at one's own pace; that pace is highly dependent on the ability of an educator to reach the student at her level and close any gaps. This became the impetus for her choosing special education as her lifelong profession.

After spending six years in the Pasadena Independent School District (outside of Houston) as a resource teacher and behavior specialist, Brionne obtained her master's degree in educational administration from Lamar University and transitioned to the role of a learning lab specialist at YES Prep Public Schools where she has been for the past four years. Presently, she is furthering her education at Rice University in Houston. She plans to open an early intervention charter school within the next few years.

Brionne is an avid reader and skilled journalist and she enjoys singing, roller skating, and spending time with her husband and son.

Evelyn Rico-Soto (formerly Rico-Hernandez) attended the University of Houston after graduating from Lamar, earning a BA in theater and literature. As an undergraduate, she studied in France with the University of Houston's Study Abroad Program and is fluent in French, English, and Spanish. An avid reader, Evelyn credits WOWU for nurturing her love of literature, a pastime she is able to enjoy in three languages. She is an active book club member and enjoys returning to Lamar each year to serve as a mentor to the new WOWU participants. She has worked as a financial counselor for the Memorial Hermann Healthcare System and in the accounting department of Memorial Hermann Hospital. Evelyn is currently completing her degree in business management at DeVry University and will continue on for her MBA at the University of Houston. She is a specialist for Cadence Trust where she manages funds for special needs trusts. Her long-term career goal is human resources or education.

Evelyn and her husband, Art, have been married for ten years and have two young sons, Ari and Eli, who have both inherited her love of reading, their favorite story being *The Gruffalo*.

ALUMNAE PROFILES

YEAR TWO

Eva Alvarado
Houston Community College

Illneisha Davis
Stephen F. Austin State University
Texas Southern University
San Jacinto College

Kamola Dolimbek
University of Houston

Christina (Gonzalez) Venegas
St. Mary's University
University of Texas

Edith Guerra Hernandez
University of Houston

Kori Hale
Hampton University
Cambridge University
Syracuse University

Delorean St. Clair Wiley
Texas A&M University
California Polytechnic

Rosalinda Sierra
University of Southern California

Zugey (Villarreal) Santacruz
University of Houston
South Texas College of Law

Chelsea Wooldridge
University of Houston

Eva Alvarado attended Houston Community College and is now married and the mother of three.

Illneisha Davis graduated from Stephen F. Austin State University in 2006. After working for Enterprise Rent a Car for almost seven years, she made a career change in 2013 to attend law school at Texas Southern University Thurgood Marshall School of Law. After her first year, Illneisha decided to pursue an associate of applied science degree in paralegal studies at San Jacinto College District and graduated in December 2015. She continues to work as a part-time educational planner at San Jacinto College North until she returns to law school in the Fall 2016.

Kamola Dolimbek graduated from the University of Houston with high honors in 2008. Kamola is now married with two children and currently works in Houston.

Christina (Gonzalez) Venegas, RN, BSN received her BA in political science from St. Mary's University in San Antonio in December 2006. She worked in administration at MD Anderson Cancer Center in Houston for five years before going back to school in 2013. Christina graduated with a BS in nursing from the University of Texas Medical Branch in Galveston in April 2014 and is now a registered nurse working at Ben Taub  General Hospital in Houston in the Surgical Intermediate Care Unit. Ultimately, she hopes to transfer to Ben Taub's Trauma Surgical ICU and, after at least two years, get accepted into a doctor of nursing practice degree program in nurse anesthesia to become a certified registered nurse anesthetist. Christina was married in June 2014, and she and her husband are now expecting their first child, a son. They plan on welcoming another one or two children into their family in the future.

Edith Guerra Hernandez attended the University of Houston majoring in education and is currently a bilingual kindergarten teacher at Humble ISD. She has been teaching for eight years. Edith is married with two young children, Kamila Isabella and Nikolas Angel.

Kori Hale graduated in 2006 with her BA in finance from Hampton University and obtained her International Business Certificate in 2007 from Cambridge University. In 2013, she graduated with her MA in broadcast and digital journalism from Syracuse University. She has been an investment analyst for UBS Investment Bank and an investment banking associate for Goldman Sachs. Kori also worked as a European television producer for Bloomberg TV and is currently a television producer for CNBC's Squawk on the Street and Squawk Alley. Additionally, she is a fashion designer. Kori currently serves on the Board of Directors of the Brooklyn Center for the Performing Arts.

Delorean St. Clair Wiley graduated from Texas A&M University in 2007 and has a master's degree in agribusiness from California Polytechnic with PMP, CSM, and ITIL certifications. She is currently a business insight analyst for Rackspace Hosting and Chair of Operations for the Professional Organization of Women at Rackspace. Delorean is married with two children, McLaren and Catalina. She and her husband recently purchased their first home on an acre of land which she hopes to expand to 20 acres for an agritourism venture.

Rosalinda Sierra studied architecture at the University of Southern California. She spent the summer of 2008 studying abroad in Japan, China, Vietnam, Cambodia, and Malaysia as part of an architecture program. Since 2012, she has been working with A-K-A Architecture + Design, an all-woman firm specializing in residential, commercial, hospitality, and interior architecture. She is currently the firm's senior project manager. Rosalinda is also an avid salsa dancer. She started salsa dancing at USC, where she then directed the school's salsa team for two years. She has since performed and taught workshops at various major salsa events across the country.

Zugey Dolores (Villarreal) Santacruz completed her undergraduate studies at the University of Houston–Main Campus in 2007 with a major in political science. She worked as a case manager for Communities in Schools at a Houston high school. Currently she is a JD candidate (May 2016) at South Texas College of Law. She and her husband, Miguel Angel, have a four year-old daughter, Ilithyia Maret.

Chelsea Wooldridge earned her Bachelor of Business Administration degree with a concentration in accounting in 2007 from the University of Houston–Main Campus and completed an internship with Ernst & Young. Instead of joining the work force immediately, she remained in college at UH and earned a Master of Science degree in Accountancy (MSACCY) in 2008. After graduation, she worked for several public accounting firms in the Houston area while studying for her CPA Exam and was officially licensed in 2011. Employed as an accountant for a local midstream oil company before transitioning out of the staff role, Chelsea began working as controller at MidCon Gathering, LLC in 2014, where she continues today. She also has been hired as an adjunct professor at Houston Community College and began teaching in the Spring 2016. Having taken an active role in WOWU, Chelsea credits the mentoring program for teaching her the importance of setting goals and for demonstrating that she is capable of excelling both personally and professionally.

> *The most important thing I learned from WOWU is that I could achieve anything—as long as I was driven to succeed and passionate about what I was doing.*
>
> *—Chelsea Wooldridge*

ALUMNAE PROFILES

YEAR THREE

Zyania Benavides
Houston Community College
University of Houston

Beatriz de Cordoba
Houston Community College
University of Houston

Jade Bonefont
Houston Community College—
West Loop
Texas Southern University

Yeiry Cristina Guevara
Ithaca College

Ashley Brantley
University of Houston
Texas Southern University
Thurgood Marshall School of Law

Leah Spurling
University of Arkansas—
Fayetteville

Jessica Cerda
University of Houston

Ashley Thomas
University of Texas at Arlington

Gaylyn Denise Crissmon
Prairie View A&M University
Houston Baptist University

Cecilia Zelaya
University of West Florida

Zyania Benavides graduated from Houston Community College with a degree in bilingual teaching and a minor in Spanish. She is currently working in the oil and gas industry with Precision Pigging, LLC, and represents the company in the USA and Mexico. Zyania was recently promoted from administration assistant to project manager. She plans on attending the University of Houston to acquire her project manager certification. Zyania has a seven year-old son, Caleb Christopher.

Jade Bonefont completed her core classes at Houston Community College and attended Texas Southern University in pursuit of a Doctor of Pharmacy degree. (Information received as of last contact.)

Ashley Brantley graduated magna cum laude from the University of Houston in 2008 with a BA in English. She is very active in WOWU and is responsible for compiling this book, the first written history of the program. She earned her Juris Doctor degree from Thurgood Marshall School of Law in 2012 and is currently a lawyer licensed in Texas and Washington, DC. Ashley has traveled to Spain, France, England, and Sweden, and has worked as a lab technician at the Karolinska Institute in Stockholm. She credits WOWU for exposing her to the arts and revealing their importance in becoming a well-rounded person.

> *The class we had with a particularly influential psychotherapist made a big impression on me. It was the first time I had heard someone say that a person is capable of molding his or her own future despite their past.*
>
> *I was shy and kind of withdrawn as a high school senior. Now when I go back and talk to the new classes of WOWU, I am reminded of how different I was then…I had no idea what I was getting into*

when I started WOWU. I remember interviewing with Mrs. Karff. I did not know the organization even existed, and I was not one of the ones originally chosen. The teachers at Lamar recommended me, and I did not know anything about Mrs. Karff or WOWU when I interviewed. I had no idea how the interview went. I was not intimidated by Mrs. Karff, but I remember really wanting to make a good impression. She has a warm sprit and I remember that from the start, but she is also a no-nonsense sort of person—someone I wanted very much to impress.

I was seventeen years old and I was nervous when she asked me about myself but she was very warm and she encouraged me to be open. I left not knowing what would happen. It was a difficult time in my life. When I go back to speak with the current ladies, I sit around that table and remember that I was very shy back then and I was going through a difficult time. My mother was and still is pretty sick, but no one knew that. Her illness had gotten progressively worse and it was very bad the year I was involved in WOWU. My mom was a very independent career woman and it was scary. I do remember that I felt nurtured in that group and I really needed it, especially at that time. I did not share what I was going through. I am a very private person, but having that very accepting group and Mrs. Karff was very comforting to me, and I remember looking forward to Thursdays and the Saturday field trips.

I always feel really excited to sit around the table when I go back to talk to the new group, which I have done every year since graduation, with the exception of my first year of law school. I think of that table as a way to gauge how far I have come. You just never know what people are going through, and I always remember that when I speak with the new ladies. People go through all sorts of things, but WOWU was, and is, a very safe and nurturing place. I was shy and stayed to myself, but my confidence grew through WOWU. I did not share what was going on at home and I was constantly worried about my mom, but WOWU was a time to focus on myself and think about the kind of woman I wanted to be. No one else asks those ques-

tions of you, especially at that age, and being concerned about my own mother and about doing well in school, I would have never asked myself those questions had Mrs. Karff not posed them. Women typically don't ask those questions until much later in life—but they're so important.

When I visit with the students, I observe that each has a career goal. Then, when I go back to the luncheon hosted by Mrs. Karff at her home, I see that these ladies actually achieve these goals. The ladies of WOWU go all over the world and do things that are really unusual and impressive. It is inspiring, and you can't underestimate the power of example. When I saw other graduates of the program on campus at U of H, it was very comforting, and we helped each other. One important thing was the constant exposure to art. I loved art and dance before, but WOWU showed me how important art was as a personal outlet for self-expression, which was hard for me back then. I joined the Latin Dance Club at Lamar High School and continued my exploration of folk dances in college by engaging in the different traditional styles of belly dance. Mrs. Karff showed me that to study and participate in the arts was a really legitimate thing. It has continued to be a really important part of my life to this day. My parents had exposed me to the arts, but Mrs. Karff helped me appreciate the arts even more.

—Ashley Brantley

Gaylyn Denise Crissmon graduated from Prairie View A&M University in 2008 with a degree in political science and a minor in English and was an assistant teacher at a private school. She is currently attending Houston Baptist University pursuing a master's degree in education. Gaylyn is married and has a daughter.

Beatriz de Cordoba attended the University of Houston—Main Campus and earned her bachelor's degree in public relations/advertisement. She is currently a sales supervisor at the clothing store Elie Tahari.

Alumnae Profiles: 2004, Year Three

Yeiry Cristina Guevara, the first from her Salvadoran-American family to attend college, graduated from Ithaca College in upstate New York in 2008 with a bachelor of science degree in business administration (dual concentrations in finance and international business, with a minor in Latin-American studies). Since graduating college, she has dedicated her professional career to the nonprofit sector, focusing on digital marketing and information management. Yeiry is currently Manager of Consultants and Programs for National Executive Services Corps (NESC), a nonprofit dedicated to empowering other nonprofits through management consulting. She is also a professional translator, freelance consultant, and writer. She resides in New York. Yeiry credits WOWU as a major influence in her life; her commitment to the program has brought her back for the year-end luncheon more than once.

> *I wouldn't be the same person if it wasn't for the skills and the character I developed as a result of WOWU.*
>
> *—Yeiry Guevara*

Zyania Benavides,
Yeiry Guevara,
and Jade Bonefant,
WOWU Class of 2004

Women on the Way Up

WOWU class at work and on field trips

ALUMNAE PROFILES

YEAR FOUR

Savannah Carter
University of St. Thomas

Alina Patricia de las Cuevas
University of Houston
Tulane University

Diana Estupiñan
University of Houston

Kimberly Figgs-Green
Lamar University

Jessica (Frederick) Brown
Baylor University
University of Texas
Southwestern Medical School

Silvia (Pejerrey) Ramirez
University of Houston—Downtown
University of St. Thomas

Kymberly Reynolds
University of Houston
Texas A&M University

Erin Robinson
Sam Houston State University

Sarah (Sanchez) Travino
Sam Houston State University

Ana Vargas
Lamar University

Alina Patricia de las Cuevas graduated from the University of Houston in December 2009 with a BS in psychology. She worked at the Bilingual Education Institute as an admissions associate for three years and completed her master's degree in finance at Tulane University in August 2013. Alina interned that summer at Koch Supply & Trading as an analyst, which led her to her current job at Noble America's Corp. as an oil liquid scheduler. There she scheduled for different trading desks with a goal of one day becoming part of the operations management team. Alina has been married to her college best friend for almost four years and enjoys time with family, friends, and their chocolate labrador Merlot. They plan on traveling before starting a family.

Kimberly Figgs-Green attended Lamar University and majored in health and kinesiology. She is married with a one year-old daughter Karleigh, and is currently a volunteer coordinator for Harris County Texas A&M Agriculture.

Jessica (Frederick) Brown, MD received her undergraduate degree from Baylor University in 2009. She then attended the University of Texas Southwestern Medical School, graduating in 2013. Jessica is married to David Brown and is currently completing her residency in obstetrics and gynecology at UTSW (Class of 2017).

Silvia Fiorela (Pejerrey) Ramirez attended the University of Houston–Downtown and is currently a Pre-K bilingual teacher for the Houston Independent School District (HISD) at Neff Elementary (ELC), a job about which she is passionate. Thanks to a scholarship she received from HISD, Sylvia is pursuing her master's degree in bilingual education at the University of St. Thomas. Silvia was married in July 2014 to her high school sweetheart of ten years and hopes to start a family soon.

Thank you for everything; for helping me to achieve my goals. With my first scholarship (from WOWU), you opened the door to new opportunities and a different life. Thank you for encouraging me to continue on my road to success.

—Silvia Pejerrey Ramirez

Alumnae Profiles: 2005, Year Four

Kymberly Reynolds is a Texas native from Houston and currently lives in Austin. She completed her undergraduate degree (BBA Finance) at the University of Houston, where she was a member of the Honors College. After graduation, Kymberly furthered her education by attending the George H.W. Bush School of Government and Public Service at Texas A&M University, where she earned a master's degree in public administration. Her professional experience is focused on management and technology consulting for a variety of federal and state healthcare programs. Outside of her professional commitments, Kymberly is active in the community, where she offers her time and talent to support initiatives that empower youth, build civic coalitions, and advance social issues. She is a proud member of Alpha Kappa Alpha Sorority, Inc., the oldest African-American Greek-letter organization for women. In September 2016, Kymberly will begin a new chapter in her life when she marries her fiancé, Brian Walton.

Erin Robinson graduated from Sam Houston State University with a BS in biology. She currently works for the Department of Energy as a safety engineer. Erin will marry Franklin Nwosu in November 2016, and her future plans include starting a family and climbing to the top in her career.

Sarah Lydia (Sanchez) Trevino graduated from Sam Houston State University in 2009 with a bachelor's degree in business administration. She interned at a Houston real estate investment company and currently works at Texas Orthopedic Hospital as an administrative assistant for the chief nursing officer and chief financial officer. Sarah is also owner of Sarah Lydia Events, a Houston, Texas based event planning company. She married in November 2015. Her long-term goal is to become a CEO or CFO in the areas of real estate investments or health care.

> *Women on the Way Up was an amazing experience. Not only did I gain knowledge about the arts, but it made me an all-around better person. This mentoring program encouraged me to set my goals high and gave me the tools to become a successful businesswoman!*
>
> *—Sarah Lydia Sanchez Trevino*

Women on the Way Up

Ana Vargas attended Lamar University in Beaumont. As a McNair Scholar, she completed research on child poverty. She also worked with a group of young women to establish the Kappa Delta Chi sorority at Lamar. Ana planned to pursue a master's degree and possibly a doctorate in social work so that she could work with impoverished populations. Ultimately, she was interested in becoming a college professor. (Information received as of last contact.)

WOWU Class of 2005

ALUMNAE PROFILES

YEAR FIVE

Icha (Nyimas) Arief
University of Houston
St. Cloud State University

Brittney Ewing
Lamar University

Renitra Fisher
University of Houston
Prairie View A&M University

Christina Guajardo
University of Houston—
Downtown
University of Texas at Austin

Carissa Jones
Sam Houston State University

Alysia Livingston
Trinity University

Claudia Martinez
University of Houston—
Downtown
Texas Woman's University

Christine Morgan
Texas A&M University—
Corpus Christi

Giselle Mugabo
Houston Community College

Linda Ojinnaka
University of Texas at
San Antonio

Icha (Nyimas) Arief graduated with her BS in psychology from the University of Houston and MS in applied behavior analysis from St. Cloud State University. She is a behavior analyst at Howry Residential Services, Inc., Mendota Heights, Minnesota.

Renitra Fisher graduated in 2011 with a Bachelor of Business Administration in management from the University of Houston–Main Campus. She obtained her Master of Business Administration from Prairie View A&M University in August 2015. Renitra is a human resources generalist at Bechtel Oil, Gas, and Chemicals.

Christina Guajardo graduated with a degree in English from the University of Houston—Downtown and has been working in clinical research at MD Anderson Cancer Center for the past ten years. She was recently admitted to the University of Texas at Austin for a graduate degree program in language and literacy, which she will begin in fall 2016.

Carissa Jones graduated from Sam Houston State and was working in property management. (Information received as of last contact.)

Claudia Martinez attended the University of Houston—Downtown and hoped to start nursing school at Texas Woman's University. Her long-range plans included obtaining a master's degree and possibly working in trauma/ER. (Information received as of last contact.)

Christine Morgan graduated from Texas A&M University with a Bachelor of Arts degree in political science. She is currently an event coordinator for the City of San Antonio and planning to begin a career as a political analyst.

Alumnae Profiles

Year Six

Frances Acevedo
University of Houston—Downtown

Maria Apreza
University of Texas at San Antonio

La Shonda Bradley
Virginia State University

Pilar Fanaselle
University of Houston

Leslie Galeas
Sam Houston State University

Seundra Gordwin
Lamar University

Nazanin Javanmardi
Houston Community College

Iryna Marchenko
Houston Community College

Shara Mills
University of Texas at Austin

Kim Loan Nguyen
We note with sadness the death of Kim Loan Nguyen, who died of leukemia in August 2007.

Women on the Way Up

Frances Acevedo graduated from the University of Houston and was employed as a pediatric oncological nurse. (Information received as of last contact.)

Maria Apreza graduated from the University of Texas at San Antonio and taught English in China. Her long-term career goals include working for the Department of State and joining the Peace Corps. Maria currently works for the Houston Rodeo.

> *I am still surprised that I have made it this far in life. I never knew that I would have the opportunity to attend a university. Now it is up to me to keep going, and hopefully, someday, I will make my dreams a reality. Thank you for giving me a little taste of the ice cream scoop. I enjoyed it.*
>
> —*Maria Apreza*

Pilar Fanaselle graduated from the University of Houston with a Bachelor of Business Administration in professional sales and marketing and a Bachelor of Business Administration in supply chain management. She is currently an inside sales representative with Insperity, Inc. demonstrating and selling products and software through interactive teleconferences. Pilar and her husband, Dan Townsend, have a baby daughter, Camilla "Cami Jo."

Leslie Galeas attended Sam Houston State University and is traveling to Nicaragua to do missionary work.

Seundra Gordwin was attending Lamar University. (Information received as of last contact.)

> *I am determined to strive as far as my success takes me.*
>
> —*Seundra Gordwin*

ALUMNAE PROFILES

YEAR SEVEN

Dominique Campbell
Xavier University of Louisiana

Bridgette Lopez
(College information not available)

Rachel Castro
University of Texas at San Antonio

Viola Rinche
Blinn College

Cassandra Fiddes
Hendrix College

Araceli Salinas
University of Houston

Janechia Jerrols
Howard University

Eliana Scuderi
(Emigrated to Argentina)

Eun Ji Lee
University of Houston

Roha Teferra
Trinity University

Rachel Castro graduated from the University of Texas at San Antonio and now works for Centerpoint Energy, one of the top north American natural gas marketers, as a derivative accountant. She volunteers and supports several organizations, including Urban Outreach, Inc., Camp of the Hills, True Vine Fellowship Heart of Zion Dance Ministry, and Inspire Women, along with other volunteer opportunities offered by her company. Rachel intends on pursuing her MBA and CPA to further her professional career. She also plans on opening a transition home for individuals who are in need of assistance in adjusting to the real world after leaving orphanages. Her hope is that the transition home will nurture responsible citizens and faithful Christians and empower them to be successful and impact the world.

My personal mission is to make an impact on the lives around me and make God famous.

—*Rachel Castro*

Alumnae Profiles

Year Eight

Shaunte Bouie
Houston Community College

Precious Byrd-Harris
Lamar University

Yessica Carrion
Houston Community College

Yesenia Chavez
University of Houston

Marilyn Ferrell
Baylor University

Karen Gallardo
University of Houston

Cristina Machado
Texas A&M University
University of Houston—
Downtown

Crystal Martinez
Northwestern University

Jacqueline Ross
Southern Methodist University

Hilda Torres
University of Evansville, Indiana
University of Haifa, Israel

Marilyn Ferrell graduated in May 2013 from Baylor University with a BA in psychology. She has been working as an acting manager at David's Bridal. Currently pursuing her graduate degree in psychology, Marilyn plans to teach at the university level and conduct research with a focus on relationship management and self actualization. She is also contemplating law school with an emphasis on equal rights and discrimination in the workplace. Marilyn enjoys reading historical nonfiction and sci-fi, keeping up with the news online, and socializing in the Houston area.

Cristina Machado graduated from Texas A&M University with honors in business and hospitality in May 2013 and worked for Hilton Hotels as an accountant. She is currently pursuing her MBA at the University of Houston—Downtown and will graduate in July 2016. Christina works for NRG Energy in fraud prevention and mitigation and hopes to move into the finance department after graduation. Her concentration is her career and education so she can help her mother and brother with whom she spends most of her time. She volunteers in the community and enjoys a healthy lifestyle.

Hilda Torres completed her undergraduate degree at the University of Evansville in Indiana, and is currently pursuing her MA in prehistoric archaeology at the University of Haifa in Israel. She will be graduating in summer 2016.

Alumnae Profiles

2010
Year Nine

Alexandra Castro
University of St. Thomas
University of Houston

Yaribey Clavel-Lobaina
University of Houston—
Honors College

Dorothy Moon
Prairie View A&M University

Yesica Moya
Houston Community College—
Southeast

Ahna Ramos
Culinary Institute LeNotre

Charkedra Randolph
University of Mary Hardin-Baylor

Katril Roberson
Lamar University

Michelle Robinson-Living
Prairie View A&M University

*Due to other commitments,
two students had to leave the
program early in 2010.*

Women on the Way Up

Alexandra Castro completed her freshman year at the University of St. Thomas before taking a gap year to work full-time. She is currently completing her BS degree in human nutrition and foods at the University of Houston. Alexandra is applying to medical school to gain admittance in fall 2017. She works at Baylor College of Medicine in the Children's Nutrition Research Center, where her job involves coordinating between researchers and the Houston community in gathering the data needed for ongoing studies.

Alexandra will be getting married in summer 2017 and is looking forward to starting a new family with her husband-to-be.

WOWU class at the Alley Theatre and at dinner following the performance

ALUMNAE PROFILES

2011
YEAR TEN

Lara Al Fady
University of St. Thomas

Cynthia Gutierrez
Houston Community College

Crystal Hernandez
University of Houston

Thu Mai Nguyen
University of Houston

Justice Owmby
Western College

Ana Perez
Houston Community College—
Central

Keandra Sharp
Houston Community College—
Southwest

Jessica Thomas
St. Edwards University

Angela Uhegwu
Prairie View A&M University

Alba Zapata
Houston Community College—
West Loop
University of Houston

Thu-Mai Nguyen holds a BS degree in kinesiology and received her BA in dance in May 2016 from the University of Houston. She plans to go into physical therapy while pursuing dance teaching.

In addition to her love of human movement, Thu-Mai is a leader in the Vietnamese youth community through numerous positions. She was the former president of the Vietnamese Student Association at UH and is the current programming director for the regional level summit for the Union of Vietnamese Student Associations of the Southern region (UVSA South). She also assists with Landmark Worldwide as a Curriculum for Living graduate in the Family Programs.

Alba Zapata is currently a student at the UH main campus and plans to major in English and minor in Spanish. Employed full-time for the Houston Independent School District and part-time for a financial firm, she thoroughly enjoys both her jobs. Alba is working toward becoming a successful teacher and is also learning about having a secure financial future. She hopes one day to succeed in having her own business in the financial industry.

Getting to where she is has not been easy. Alba's mother passed away at a young age, and she has tried her best to be there for her five younger siblings and also to be a good role model for them all. Karate is her biggest passion. Having trained in karate since she was four years old, Alba is now a black belt and has competed at an international level.

Alba and her fiancé are currently in the process of finding their first dream home and planning their wedding.

Women on the Way Up opened my eyes to so many different things. It was a wonderful opportunity and a great learning experience.

–Alba Zapata

Alumnae Profiles

2012
Year Eleven

Leslie Aikens
Texas A&M University—
Corpus Christi

Elizabeth Allen
University of Houston

Tiffani Boston
Texas Southern University
Baylor Medical School

Erica Brooks
Texas Tech University

Nhi Dinh
Earlham College
Richmond, Indiana

Chardonae Givens
University of Houston

Selina Khwaja
University of Texas at Austin

Carmin Munoz-Lavanderos
Columbia University

Tania Tong
Texas A&M University

Tytiana Wilson
Lamar University

Tiffani Boston graduated from Texas Southern University in May 2016 with a major in biology. She is pursuing a career path in the health profession of psychiatry and plans to pursue her medical degree at Baylor Medical School. Tiffani was born and raised in Houston and is the second oldest of four children. Coming together as a family is extremely important to her.

The WOWU program is extremely optimistic. It really shows young ladies that it's okay to make it to the top and it encourages us to strive to reach our fullest potential. It has been excellent in helping to develop intellect and in exposing us to the world beyond what 'we' young women see. It has opened our eyes to things that we did not have the chance to participate in because of family finances.

I believe that more mentoring programs would help shy people to find a voice of their own. The balance between someone with a strong personality and someone with a weak one is to help each other. The world promotes competition with one another, but why not help and reach out to those who need it the most? This program really brings out the best in the individual. If there were mentoring programs all across the world, I feel that the percentage of high school students continuing on to college would increase.

I am very honored to say that I am a 2012 WOWU graduate. Mrs. Karff did an amazing job of exposing me to information and opportunities I didn't know existed. This is a much-needed course for most students because I learned things far beyond my core class curriculum. I am very honored that I was chosen from a group of roughly fifty young ladies to be a part of this amazing class. I thank and commend Mrs. Karff for starting and continuing this exquisite program called WOWU.

–Tiffani Boston

ALUMNAE PROFILES

2013
YEAR TWELVE

Marlen Benitez
University of St. Thomas

Laura Cowling
(College information not available)

Marisol Guerrero
Houston Community College

Jennifer Gutierrez
Baylor University

Inga Irving
Blinn College

Tyler Mims
University of Houston at San Antonio

Anna Maria Morris
Sam Houston State University

Daniella Recio
Texas A&M University

Abetzi Reyes
University of Houston

Antonella Rodriguez
Houston Community College

Elizabeth Trujillo
University of Houston

Due to the exceptional nature of the candidate pool, a decision was made to admit an additional student to the WOWU program in 2013.

Marlen Benitez is majoring in biology at the University of St. Thomas (Class of 2017) with a focus on pre-med and a minor in international studies. Her goal is to become a pediatric emergency room doctor/surgeon with hopes of traveling to developing countries to assist in enhancing their health care systems. Marlen's family is originally from Mexico. She was born in the Uinted States and is a first-generation college student.

Tyler Mims graduated summa cum laude from the University of Houston in December 2016 and is currently a legal assistant. She plans on attending law school in fall 2017.

Anna Maria Morris is currently a junior at Sam Houston State University studying theatre with an emphasis in acting and directing. She is very involved in the theatre department at the university and works part-time in the University Theatre Center Box Office as a box office attendant and assistant to the house manager. Anna was an ensemble member in *"Machinal,"* an award-winning play performed at the Kennedy Center as part of the American College Theatre Festival. She is also a member of the Honors College and the Alpha Lambda Delta National Honors Society. After graduation, she plans to pursue a career in theatre. Anna is very close with her supportive family, including her three sisters, all of whom are attending college.

Alumnae Profiles

2014
Year Thirteen

Dhanisha Balsara
University of Houston

Cierra Duckworth
Rice University

Charlie-Anne Gagne
University of Houston—
Honors College

Fryda Gonzalez
University of Houston

Doris Hui
University of Texas at Austin

Anxhela Hysi
Houston Community College

Genesis Larin
Baylor University

Rachel Massey
Bryn Mawr College

Brianna McGowan
University of Texas at
Arlington

Lissette Morejon
University of Houston

Dhanisha Balsara is a sophomore at the University of Houston majoring in accounting. She is a volunteer at the Houston Humane Society and Houston Food Bank. Dhanisha plans on becoming a CPA.

> *I truly believe that I view the world differently due to the experiences I have gained through the Women on The Way Up program. I appreciate everything that Ms. Karff did and is still doing.*
>
> *– Dhanisha Balsara*

Charlie-Anne Gagne is pursuing her BA in psychology with a minor in honors creative works at the University of Houston Honors College, where she will likely graduate early. Interested in widening her world view and shaping her political self, her classes include women's studies and representing Islam. Charlie-Anne has worked at the Houston Zoo and also as a sales associate at a speciality goods store. She recently spent a month visiting her ailing grandmother in Quebec, Canada, in preparation for writing her memoir. Charlie-Anne's family is very involved in community events.

Doris Hui is currently attending the University of Texas at Austin majoring in economics and minoring in computer science. She has been working for Apple as an AppleCare advisor since June 2015, and as a web development associate at UT Austin's School of Undergraduate Studies since January 2016.

Genesis Larin is currently a sophomore at Baylor University (Class of 2018) majoring in English literature with a minor in sociology.

> *The Women on the Way Up program has provided me with cultural information I continue to use today. I had some of the best experiences with Mrs. Karff as well as my fellow peers in the program. Since the program, I am more conscious of the fine arts. I am forever thankful to Mrs. Karff for giving me the opportunity to be a part of her program.*
>
> *– Genesis Larin*

Alumnae Profiles

2015
Year Fourteen

Jessica Arrozola
St. Edward's University
Austin

Mikoto Brunet
Texas Woman's University

Jennifer Gray
Brandeis University

Michelle Huynh
University of Houston

Natachi Iheanacho
University of Texas at
San Antonio

Maci Kelley
Sam Houston State University

Daniela Sofia Lopez
Bryn Mawr College

Aina Shiver
Houston Community College

Madeline Uraih
Johns Hopkins

Alexandra Venegas
Texas A&M University

Jennifer Gray is currently attending Brandeis University (Class of 2019), pursuing a double major in Neuroscience and Business, as well as a creative writing and computer science double minor. Jennifer credits the love, strength, and full support of her family for her success and also as her inspiration as she continues her college career.

Michelle Huynh is majoring in biology at the University of Houston. She plans on pursuing a career as a pharmacist or a physician's assistant.

Maci Kelley is an only child and first-generation college student who was raised in a single-parent household by her mother. She is currently a mathematics, bachelor of science major at Sam Houston State University, with hopes of becoming an actuary. Maci plans to transfer to the University of Houston–Main Campus, where she will complete her degree.

Daniela Sofia Lopez, an undergraduate student at Bryn Mawr College (Class of 2019), is an aspiring international human rights lawyer.

Alexandra Venegas is currently a freshman at Texas A&M University majoring in communication and double minoring in Spanish and business administration.

CURRENT CLASS

2016
YEAR FIFTEEN

Lisbeth Arriola

Sara Dalalzahed

Elizabeth Dang

Kameron John

Adrianna Leveston

Melissa Lopez

Christine Njoku

Ashley Nkrumah

Blanca Pompa

One student had to leave the program early in 2016.

Lisbeth Arriola, a member of the current Women on the Way Up class, plans to attend the University of Houston—Downtown after graduation from Lamar High School. Undecided on her long-term career path, Lisbeth is hoping to major either in biology or in psychology to become an occupational therapist.

Sara Dalalzahed will study biology at the University of Houston—Downtown and plans to attend medical school to study dermatology.

Elizabeth Dang will be attending the University of Houston to pursue a career in chemical engineering. She hopes to help develop renewable energy and make it more affordable and easier to use.

Adrianna Leveston plans to pursue general studies for a year at the University of Texas at Arlington and then transfer to the University of Texas at Austin to follow its pre-med curriculum. She ultimately hopes to attend medical school and become a psychiatrist. Adrianna's goal is to open her own business once she completes her residency requirements.

> *Mrs. Karff allowed so many opportunities. One of the major impacts was her ability to fund a $1,000 scholarship. The money helps me tremendously.*
>
> *She also broadened my view of the arts, especially dance. The lessons and field trips we took allowed me to expand whatever knowledge I had prior to Women on the Way Up. Mrs. Karff also provided a basic expectation of how to utilize the world to make it my own.*
>
> *– Adrianna Leveston*

Melissa Lopez will be studying civil engineering at the University of Houston after graduating from Lamar High School.

Alumnae Profiles: 2016, Year Fifteen

Christine Njoku will be attending Howard University in the fall to study health sciences.

> *Mrs. Karff allowed me to unlock the unconventional side of knowledge that is often neglected in typical classes. She helped me to become a more well-rounded woman and opened my eyes to the beauty of all types of art.*
>
> *– Christine Njoku*

Ashley Nkrumah is proud to announce that she will be attending the University of Texas at San Antonio, where she will be pursing a career in nursing to become a nurse practitioner.

> *This year I enjoyed participating in Women on the Way Up, where I learned and experienced so much to help me be a successful young lady in my future.*
>
> *– Ashley Nkrumah*

Blanca Pompa is passionate about optometry and plans to pursue that field of study.

> *I think Mrs. Karff really opened up the idea of being well involved, not just in academics, but also in the arts, and so, because of the program, I think I'll also end up doing something art related in the next few years.*
>
> *– Blanca Pompa*

> *The program is a good step up the ladder. Some of the students have come a long way by being the first in their families to attend and finish college. I feel very proud to have taken part in this endeavor, but my role was small. Joan Karff did most of the work.*
>
> —**Ray Reiner**
> **President, WOWU Board**

WOWU class of 2016 at Brennan's following the Houston Ballet performance

A Message from Joan Karff

*I*t is my hope that there will be some readers who will be inspired to duplicate "Women on the Way Up" in their own communities. The main outlines of this mentoring program have been delineated for easy replication, but it is important to note that the interests and talents of the individual group leader can shape the program content. Those sections of the program which are outside of the expertise of the leader can be handled by guest speakers in the community. I have used guests to explore the fine points of classical music before our field trip to the symphony, and I have relied on young minority women doctors and lawyers to come and talk about their careers. The crucial message of this mentoring program is to expand horizons of underprivileged young women, and there are many paths to achieving this goal.

> *This is a program that is 100% effective. Period. I can't think of another program that has this success year after year. Ten students for fifteen years have succeeded in completing college, graduate school often, and these are not the students who were expected to do these things. These are students who had the odds against them, but had the desire to succeed.*
>
> **—Dr. James McSwain,**
> **Principal, Lamar High School**

> WoWU demonstrates that a mentoring program can facilitate enormous emotional, intellectual, and social growth, and provide young women with the tools needed to be effective advocates for themselves by expanding their worldview and challenging them to examine their assumptions. It is a constellation of experiences that help students find an internal compass and the courage to persevere.
>
> —*Laura Sheinkopf*

Appendix

Content Objectives for a Yearlong, Small-Group Mentoring Program

Joan Karff has designed a curriculum that she hopes will be intellectually and emotionally challenging for participants. She also has created classes that have a strong practical component. WOWU's curricular goals are based on weekly, ninety-minute sessions and a handful of field trips. The following is a summary of the program's objectives:

1. **Current events discussions:** At least two sessions require the students to read and review important news stories from the press, the Internet, and television newscasts beforehand. They report on these news items to the class and prepare answers for potential questions that may arise during the discussion.

    The current events segment helps the young women to understand the historical nature of conflicts now occurring in volatile regions of the world. The discussion of contemporary social issues serves to define each student's feelings about sensitive subjects, such as gay marriage and abortion rights.

2. **Art history:** Three sessions focus on a sampling of art, from its earliest cave-wall manifestations through antiquity, the Medieval and Renaissance periods, and into the beginnings of the modern era in France and the United States. These sessions culminate in a docent-led visit to Houston's Museum of Fine Arts.

    The segment on art history illustrates the universal quest for self-expression. The class comes to understand the line between art and religion in the Middle Ages and Renaissance, and observes the transformation from decorative and ornate as Europe experiences a more populist political force.

3. **History of dance:** There are three sessions where students learn sequences containing rhythm and movement ideas of folk dance, courtly dance, classical ballet, and modern dance. Appropriate music helps to illuminate these small sample dances. The students learn a facsimile of an early percussive rain dance, and they are taught the steps to an authentic group dance. In addition, they learn to do a stately minuet and discover how the grace and formality expressed by this style of dance laid the foundations of classical ballet. Finally, they try some of the more angular elements of pioneering Martha Graham's modern dance. WOWU members attend a Houston dance event at the completion of these classes.

4. **Introduction to classical music:** The students discuss the differences between serious eighteenth-century musical forms and current-day popular music. They look into the structure of the classical music they will hear at the Houston Symphony, as well as the composers featured at the concert.

5. **Theater as artistic expression:** The students explore the need to create dramatic representations of our world with a discussion of the role of theater in America. Reading *Our Town* and sampling the magic of pretending to be another character precede a field trip to a Houston live-theater performance.

6. **Guest speakers:** Women in the community who have achieved success in a variety of fields are invited to speak about their accomplishments. Featured speakers come from backgrounds that are similar to those of the students, making their journeys more inspiring and relevant to WOWU participants. Guest speakers are interspersed throughout the year with the sessions on the arts. The students are eager to know how college studies compare with high school. They ask about the GREs, the LSATs, and MCATs and how to balance studying with holding down a job. They are very curious about the financial indebtedness incurred with college and graduate school. In each instance, the guests have been helpful and generous with their responses.

Appendix: Content Objectives

7. **Oral reports:** Each student is required to do extra reading on the life and contributions of an important contemporary or historical woman. Some of the women who have been covered in recent years include Condoleezza Rice, Eva Perón, Judith Jamison, and Aung San Suu Kyi.

8. **Book reports:** Each student is required to write two book reports, one in late fall and one in early spring, on books selected from a reading list (see sample list). The books must be easily accessible and inspirational to young women.

9. **Practical wisdom:** The students are urged to develop an appreciation for the importance of money management, parenting skills, and self-awareness.

Money Management: The WOWU participants prepare a personal budget by deciding how, when they are first earning a paycheck, they will allocate it. They are asked to divide a hypothetical $2,000 monthly paycheck between rent, transportation, insurance, food, entertainment, and other expenses. Young women often fail to realize that expenses, such as vet bills or Christmas gifts, can make a huge dent in the budget. In addition, the class talks about the pitfalls of credit card fees and the necessity of avoiding interest and penalties.

Parenting Skills: As the majority of young women will become parents, healthy ways of parenting are discussed. This class begins with an honest appraisal of "How were you raised?" The students are frank about what they would replicate and what they would avoid when they assess the roles of their mothers and fathers in raising them. The class is asked to think about the challenge of instilling independence in a child when a parent is also concerned about the safety of that child. They are questioned about sibling rivalry and manifestations of favoritism. They list those attributes which they hope to encourage in a child and then talk about the ways to help foster these attitudes.

Women on the Way Up

BOOK REPORTS

Reports must include detailed character descriptions, a clear account of the plot, and an explanation of how the book chosen relates to them specifically. The WOWU reading list is eclectic and ever-changing, comprised of both fiction and non-fiction. The following are some recent selections:

Reading List

Kaffir Boy by Mark Mathabane: the true tale of growing up poor during the apartheid years in South Africa, using tennis as a path toward education and a better life.

The Kite Runner by Khaled Hosseini: a brilliant story of life in Afghanistan and the turmoil of one boy whose life is shaped by tumultuous political changes in his country.

The Glass Castle by Jeannette Walls: a memoir about an intelligent girl whose eccentric parents choose to live a life free of all material comforts.

Left to Tell by Immaculée Ilibagiza: the brutal 1994 tribal war in Rwanda, narrated by a sensitive and brave survivor.

The Post-Office Girl by Stefan Zweig: this superbly written tale focuses on the life of a poor Austrian girl coming of age between the two great wars. She gets a glimpse of what life is like for the privileged elite, but must return to her meager and unhappy existence.

Other selections:
Atonement by Ian McEwan
The Road to Coorain by Jill Ker Conway
Heaven Lake by John Dalton
When I Was Puerto Rican by Esmeralda Santiago
The Secret Life of Bees by Sue Monk Kidd
Pretty Birds by Scott Simon
All But My Life by Gerda Klein
Infidel by Ayaan Hirsi Ali

Appendix: Content Objectives

Without a Map by Meredith Hall
Three Cups of Tea by Greg Mortenson
Unaccustomed Earth by Jhumpa Lahiri
Loving Frank by Nancy Horan
Snowflower and the Secret Fan by Lisa See
Swallow the Ocean by Laura Flynn

DAY IN THE LIFE

Karff's program takes full advantage of her experience working with small groups of young women, as well as her connections to various Houston-based organizations and individuals who provide content for the sessions. What follows are a few examples of these sessions, which she has titled "A Day in the Life."

Law

Karff's daughter, Amy Karff Halevy, a partner in the law firm of Bracewell, LLP (a leading law and government relations firm), has spoken to the students about being an attorney and how to have a career in law. She also has worked with the students on their public speaking assignment. As part of this assignment, each student is tasked with making an oral presentation to the class. After the presentation, the student is critiqued and given positive and constructive feedback. The goal of the assignment is to help the students feel more comfortable speaking publicly and to understand the importance of that skill. Halevy also involved a young lawyer, Tamara Stiner Toomer, who has become an enthusiastic supporter of WOWU, eventually serving on the board of directors. Ms. Toomer speaks to the group about her experiences as an African-American woman and fellow graduate of Lamar High School. Ms. Toomer's impressive background includes degrees in chemical engineering, law, and business. She discusses how she was able to evaluate her skills and interests as she weighed various career options.

Music

Each year, Karff has cultural historian, Ira J. Black, and technical musician, Dr. Gary Patterson, prepare the students for a trip to hear the Houston Symphony Orchestra. Black is an engaging and wildly popular Houston Community College professor who lectures on musicology, public speaking, theater, and related topics. He also has served as commentator for the Houston Symphony. Before the field trip, Black gives a lecture to establish a historical context for the musical works they will hear. The students are given a capsule view of the history of the composers. They also are told about the specific instruments in each section of the orchestra and how these instruments are utilized by the composer.

Architecture

Karff turned to an old friend and retired architect to find a female architect who could share her experiences with the WOWU students. She found an ideal representative in Nicola Springer, an African-American woman who attended Princeton on an athletic scholarship. A native of Barbados, Springer worked for Kirksey Architecture in Houston and is a member of the Rice Design Alliance. She dazzles students each year with a presentation that includes architectural drawings and complex computer renderings.

Medicine

Although medicine is a popular career aspiration, Karff knows that many young people do not fully understand the demands of a career in this field. Karff invited a young African-American woman, a resident at Baylor Clinic, to visit the class for the first three years of WOWU. After that resident left Houston, Karff has continued to find other female medical students or residents who are willing to share the evolution of their aspirations and the specifics of their training with WOWU students.

Appendix: Content Objectives

Psychotherapy

Karff's daughter, Liz Karff Seitz, a Licensed Master Social Worker and an Advanced Clinical Practitioner (LMSW-ACP) with more than two decades of experience, has a private practice specializing in couples work. Honest and direct, Seitz never fails to elicit laughter with her compassionate and incisive presentations. Each year, she visits the class and encourages open conversation about a range of personal issues, which almost always include the students' desire for independence and the frustration they feel at being denied the freedoms that their male counterparts seem to enjoy. The sessions frequently elicit stories about single mothers who fear their daughters will make similar mistakes, and who are, as a result, deeply protective. Seitz also covers topics such as sibling rivalry, angry parents, and conflicts with boyfriends. She discusses sensitive issues including trust and openness, and she urges the young ladies to seek professional help if and when problems overwhelm them.

Theater

Karff has made use of a variety of renowned Houston cultural institutions, including the Alley Theatre, one of the largest nonprofit theaters in the United States. The company has a well-regarded outreach and education program, and each year a member visits the WOWU class and discusses everything from lighting and makeup design to the demands of being a member of a company that produces new productions every year. The content of these sessions varies depending on the speaker; some theater members have brought scripts for the group to perform. Karff also introduces the work of great American playwrights and discusses the ways in which the dramatic arts reveal important aspects of the American experience.

Job Etiquette

Karff wants WOWU students to receive concrete instruction on how to present themselves in interviews. Each year she invites an etiquette instructor and Rice University students to visit the group. During these sessions, the instructor talks about proper dress, eye contact, posture, and diction when meeting a prospective employer. The group discusses résumé writing and how to answer some of the more common interview questions. The participants learn the importance of basic—but often overlooked—behaviors, such as a firm handshake and standing when the interviewer enters the room. The goal is to make students aware of the proper way to present themselves in interviews.

Alumnae Days

Each time one of my WOWU young ladies tells me she is getting married, I hope that the person she has chosen will be generous of spirit, open to new things, and on the path with her to a life of fullness.

—*Joan Karff*

Alumnae gatherings are opportunities for current students to hear from past participants. Their stories are honest and reveal the hard work that has led to success. These presentations are a chance for Karff to convey to her students that she is just as proud of the way they have navigated various challenges as she is of their accomplishments.

Karff's home is filled with artifacts from her rich and interesting life, revealing a woman who has found a way to honor her past by making its most important lessons the reason for her current work. Students are invited to write on the walls of a designated room in the Karff home with permanent markers; this sanctioned graffiti has become a WOWU tradition. The walls are filled with comments from an ever-widening sorority of young women who were fortunate enough to have had a mentor who handed each of them a pen and gave them permission to write on the walls.

SAMPLE SYLLABUS

The following is a sample syllabus from the 2012–2013 year of WOWU:

Sept 20: Introduction. What is your personal history? What are the goals of this program? Current events assignments will be given out.

Sept 27: Discussion of current events.

Oct 4: Continuation of current events.

Oct 11: Guest speaker, Tamara Toomer: Choosing law as a profession. Assignment for next week: What in your life might be used as a theme for a play?

Oct 18: Theater in America. Reading from the script of *Our Town*. Discuss own ideas for a play.

Oct 25: Guest from Alley Theatre. Talk about the classic American drama, *Death of a Salesman*, by Arthur Miller.

Sunday, Oct 28: FIELD TRIP TO THE ALLEY THEATRE. Meet at east side between 1 p.m. and 1:15 p.m. Bus leaves promptly at 1:15 p.m. Dinner will follow the theater.

Nov 1: Art History I. Exploring the art of primitive peoples and the creativity of ancient Near East, Egypt, Greece, and Rome.

Nov 8: Art in the early Christian world. Great works of Medieval and Renaissance Europe with a focus on Italy.

Nov 15: Art in a secular age. Modern innovations in Impressionism, Cubism, and Expressionism.

Nov 17: SATURDAY FIELD TRIP TO THE MUSEUM OF FINE ARTS. Bus leaves east side at 1:15 p.m. Light meal following.

Thursday, Nov 22: OFF FOR THANKSGIVING.

Nov 29: Guest speaker on medicine as a career. First book report due. Describe plot, character development, and how your life experience helps you understand this book. Give quotes from the book.

Dec 6: Money management and budgeting.

December 22–January 7: OFF FOR CHRISTMAS BREAK.

Jan 10: Importance of solid parenting skills. Bring an art project (a sample of one of the art styles discussed).

Jan 17: Architecture as a career (guest speaker).

Jan 24: Understanding classical music: Ira J. Black. The life and times of Mahler and Mendelssohn.

Jan 31: Experiencing a symphony concert: Dr. Gary Patterson.

February 3: SUNDAY FIELD TRIP TO THE HOUSTON SYMPHONY. 1:15 p.m. departure from east side. No late seating.

Feb 7: Alumnae Day. Graduates of WOWU will speak.

Feb 14: Dance History I. How did early civilizations incorporate dance into their lives?

Feb 21: Dances of the Medieval European Court. The beginning of classical ballet.

Feb 28: Modern Dance Pioneers: Isadora Duncan and Martha Graham.

March 3: SUNDAY FIELD TRIP TO HOUSTON BALLET for production of *La Bayadere*. Be at east side at 12:45!!

March 11–March 15: OFF FOR SPRING BREAK.

Mar 21: Oral Reports. Each will have been assigned a famous woman to research and speak about. Last book report due.

Mar 28: Guest speaker, psychotherapist Liz Seitz: Personal problems and relationship issues.

Apr 4: Continuation of Liz Seitz discussion.

Apr 11: Last session and final evaluation.

Dinner at Café M at Lamar with your families (date to be announced).

Luncheon at Joan Karff's house (date to be announced).

Women on the way Up

LEADERSHIP & BOARD

LEADERSHIP

Ray Reiner
BOARD PRESIDENT
rsreiner@hotmail.com

Dr. Gary Patterson
LAMAR COORDINATOR
gpatters@houstonisd.org

Joan Karff
DIRECTOR
joankarff@usa.net

Dr. James McSwain
PRINCIPAL, LAMAR HIGH SCHOOL

BOARD OF DIRECTORS

Ray Reiner
Dr. Gary Patterson
Tamara Stiner
Ashley Brantley

Women on the way Up